JOAN
What's-Her-Name?

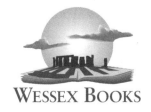

WESSEX BOOKS

Published in Great Britain by Wessex Books
2 Station Cottages, Newton Toney, Salisbury, Wiltshire SP4 0HD

First published 2002

ISBN 1-903035-10-4

Typeset in Perpetua
Printed and bound in Great Britain by Thruxton Press, Andover, Hants

To my sister Joy,
the only person who understands me

CONTENTS

Family portrait, 3rd September, 1939

PART ONE

1933—40

My parents

IF YOU'RE HOPING TO READ A BOOK CONTAINING EXPLICIT SEX, MURDER or Sci-Fi, this is not for you! As I was growing up in the 1940s I can only recall sex as something done by boys, men, married ladies and bad girls. The war was in full swing so I don't recall murders, and Sci-Fi hadn't been invented. If any of these categories are your 'thing' then put me back on the shelf to avoid disappointment.

This is a true story about how my life was turned upside down by circumstances beyond my control. I begin with a kaleidoscope of early memories and like the majority of children I can't be definite about days, months or years, until one day something terrible happens. Then you search your mind for happy thoughts to sustain you through the bad times and everything becomes as clear as yesterday, staying in the mind for the rest of your life.

I was born in Woolwich Military Hospital in London at 04.15 on 6 April 1933, the third child of George and Dora Silver. The other two children were my sister Joy, aged two, and my brother David, whose first birthday was the day before I arrived, a lovely birthday present for him! I took my Mother by surprise, so instead of walking up the hill to the hospital as she'd planned, she had to go by ambulance, the ambulance man carried her by the arms and shoulders while my Father carried her legs. Mother concentrated on keeping me in her knickers! If I'd known what the future held in store for me I wouldn't have been in such a hurry to arrive. My younger brother, Gerald, was born seventeen months later.

Woolwich

In April 1935 my Father, a regular soldier in the Royal Artillery, was posted to Port Royal in Jamaica. We had two wooden houses with verandahs as the quarters were not large enough for a family of four children; we lived in one quarter and slept in the other. Opposite the quarters was a row of huts for the locals, and in between, a dirt road. Directly opposite our quarters was a row of native huts and in one of these lived Cassie. She and her partner had six children and were saving up to be married. She looked after

Cassie

King George V dies

us while my Mother was at her meetings with the Mothers' Union and Temperance, Mother was very strong on temperance as she had grown up with the problems that drink can cause in a family. I didn't go to school, I was only three at the time, but Joy and David being older did go to school. I can remember taking biscuits to the school and passing them through the railings of the playground and wishing I too could go to school. In the hot months my Father hired the NAAFI (Navy, Army and Air Force Families Institute) donkey, he would strap tea chests to either side of the donkey like panniers, for the youngest children to sit in, while the two older children walked or sat astride its back when they were tired. We would make our way up into the hills where the air was cooler, and holiday in a place called Newcastle. In Port Royal we would swim in the sea but had to beware of the crabs hiding in the sand waiting to nip our toes. There was a barrier across the mouth of the bay to protect us from the encircling sharks.

My Father was stationed in the fort at Port Royal where Nelson once stayed, and it was rumoured that there was a ghost who could sometimes be seen in the shaded corner. It was very scary for a three year old, but not quite as frightening as the noise of the cannons firing out to sea on the day King George V died. I had to put my fingers in my ears to shut out the 'boom'. There was a house near the quarters which we were forbidden to approach. Half of it had sunk into the ground while the other half was sticking up in the air. This was caused by an earthquake years before. It was made of brick and inside it smelt horrible. Being a child, and children are known for doing the opposite of what they're told, I went in. Too late I realised it was too steep to climb out again (proving that parents do know best!) My Father had to rescue me and was very cross. The only other time I made him angry was when a friend and I played

'hairdressers'. While eating my soup at dinner time I kept pulling hairs out of my mouth. They were falling from the serrated edges of what had been my fringe.

For a treat, if we slept in the afternoon with my Dad we could stay up after dark. I can remember lying under the mosquito net pretending to be asleep and not daring to move. The reward was a magical experience. I watched the lobster fishermen walk up the road with their catch, each carrying a lantern. It was very dark and the light from their lanterns would snake into the distance as they made their way home. It was well worth a siesta. Another magical experience was a fancy dress parade (perhaps for the Coronation of King George VI). I can't remember the costumes of my elder siblings but I was dressed as a nurse and Gerald (still a baby) represented Cupid. He wasn't very happy about being so scantily dressed in public with a cocoa tin wrapped in silver paper slung across his chest to hold his arrows. A game my Father

played with us four children was 'horse-racing'. He would have a piece of paper on the table, draw four lines lengthways and write our names at the top of each column; he'd then start a spark with the end of his cigarette, the winner was the spark that got to the top of the page first; there was no reward, just the delight of winning. My Father also started us all stamp collecting at an early age. We each had our own album and there was a great deal of rivalry. He was a heavy smoker and he collected Gallaher cigarette cards, putting them carefully into sets in his album.

My earliest memory of pain was when we decided to use the bed as a trampoline. It had an iron headboard from which we took turns to leap onto the metal springs, we then rolled off the bed and ran round to have another turn. Unfortunately, due to mis-timing, somebody landed on my collar bone. Moth-

er was not amused! Neither was I when she put me in my younger brother's pushchair to wheel me to the local doctor. I did a lot of screaming while he put wads of cotton wool on my elbow, fixed my arm in a sling and told me it was a 'dolly'. On the way home we went to the NAAFI shop, Mother sat me on the counter and a man gave me a free lollipop for being a good girl ... undeserved!

We returned to England during November 1937 on RMS *Oropesa*. I don't remember anything about the journey back to England or life on board ship but I do have a copy of a menu for a children's tea party, dated 18 November 1937.

THIRD CLASS.

Breakfast

Oatmeal Porridge

Fried Egg

Grilled Smoked Bacon

Saute Potatoes

Fresh Bread · Marmalade

Tea Coffee

Dinner

Scotch Broth

Roast Quarters of Lamb, Mint Sauce

Green Peas Boiled and Browned Potatoes

Plum Pudding, Sweet Sauce

T e a

Preserved Salmon with Lettuce

Cold Meat Pickles

Currant Buns

Dessert Apples

Tea Fresh Bread Butter

Milk Pudding obtainable daily for Children on request

R.M.S. 7th November,

" OROPESA." 1937.

Consomme made by Pixies

Creme made by Elves

Percy Plaice with Butter

Susie Sunshine Sausages

Jack-and-the-Beanstalk Cutlets

Cheerful Charlie Cauliflower

Potatoes mashed by Merlin's magic

Cold Buffet

Here's a chick, there's a chick (chicken)

The pig that Tom stole (Ham)

Pancakes made by Peter Pan

Red Riding Hood Jelly Creams

Jig-saw Fruit Salad

Queen of Hearts' Tarts and Pastries

Bang-Bang Crackers

Fairy's Fresh Fruit

I do recall the fun of standing on deck and 'smoke' coming from our mouths, just like Dad when he smoked his cigarettes. This was my first recollection of cold weather.

Southsea

My Father's next posting was to Southsea in Hampshire and we lived in quarters inside the barracks. I remember the interior of the quarter was dark and gloomy with very small windows and brown paint everywhere, it was very high up and we had to climb the stairs each time we went out or returned home, there were no lifts. The stairs were metal and made a lovely cluncking sound as we stomped up and down. An advantage was, we could hear if anyone was visiting long before they arrived at the door.

Army school

I started my education at the army school in the barracks. We sat in straight rows at our desks and had slates to write on with pieces of chalk. From day one we started lessons. We had our own 'sum-sheets' and each child worked at his, or her, own pace, allowing the more gifted children to forge ahead and the less able not to feel disheartened. I shall be forever thankful to the army for their good educational grounding.

The Dentist

One thing I was not grateful for was a lasting fear of the dentist. My Mother would take me to a large Victorian building, (everything's large when you're small) where we'd climb up several flights of stairs before entering a long room with lines of dentists' chairs as far as the eye could see, and the only sound was the grinding of the drills.

We often had days out at Southsea fair, Joy and I wearing identical Panama hats, and dresses with smocked bodices (my Mother was very proud of her smocking). Sometimes it seemed as if I was wearing the same dress for ever, as I would inherit Joy's dress when she had grown out of it, I used to hate that! For an extra treat we'd have a ride on the miniature railway, it was great fun sitting in the open carriages and pretending we were on a real train. Aunt Edie and Aunt Marie (my Father's sisters), both spinsters at the time, arrived from London wearing their pyjamas, or so we children thought, we didn't know it was the 'height of London fashion'. They became friendly with a couple of fellows at the fair and they'd bring us rag dolls and tins of 'Bluebird' toffees. On Sunday mornings, my Father would take us to watch the Military Bands and afterwards he'd buy us an ice cream in the shop in the Guildhall Square. We would have a penny cornet each and he'd have a tuppeny wafer, I wanted a wafer but was told to wait until I was grown up. We'd walk in the gardens at the back of the Guildhall to see if the peacock would spread his tail … what a lovely sight when he did!.

I used to have trouble with styes on my eyes, they were red and swollen and the nurse would come to the quarter each morning to put 'Golden eye ointment' on them with the end of a matchstick.

I contracted scarlet fever and was sent to the isolation hospital for a month, (my sister was already there). It smelt of carbolic and to make matters worse I was put into a cot (a five year old in a cot!). Mum and Dad visited me but they had to stand behind glass doors at the end of the ward and wave. The other thing I remember during my stay was tapioca pudding … every day! I would try to eat the bits in between the lumps, until a young lad sat opposite me one day and said he loved tapioca pudding. He cleared my plate for me each day from then on. After four weeks in the ward I was taken one evening to a communal bathroom, it had stone floors, white tiles and duckboards to stand on. I was thoroughly scrubbed in carbolic before going to bed and the next morning I was allowed to go home. It was the day of the children's Christmas party but I wasn't allowed to go, so my Father bought me home the fairy from the top of the Christmas tree.

Scarlet fever

One morning I looked down from the quarters' windows and saw an unforgettable sight. There was a regiment of Scotsmen playing their bagpipes, their tartan kilts swinging as they marched out of the barrack gates, it was a memorable moment. Mother said they were going to the war.

I don't know what I was suffering from, maybe it was measles, but I can't remember, and I was sent to convalesce with an aunt who lived in Leighton Buzzard. She had a cottage in the middle of nowhere and lived with her husband and only son, Clifford. I had my first experience of eating porridge with salt instead of sugar, it was awful! My Aunt insisted it was the proper way to serve porridge and to have sugar on it would spoil the taste. I wasn't convinced. Aunt Edie came to visit me from London and for a treat took me to see the new Walt Disney film *Snow White and the Seven Dwarfs*. I was very scared by the wicked queen, but laughed at the antics of the Seven Dwarfs and soon learnt to sing 'Heigh-Ho, Heigh-Ho, it's off to work we go'. That night I stayed in London with my Grandmother Silver. Her family had left Ireland during the potato famine and settled in Essex when she was still a small child. She now lived with my Aunt in a tall block of flats in Greenwich. It didn't look very inviting from the outside; washing was hanging out to dry on the verandahs and the whole area had an air of poverty about it. Inside it was different though, she made me most welcome and was genuinely pleased to see me. She wore black boots, but one boot was made higher to correct the fact that one leg was shorter than the other. I was told that her foot became crippled when she fell from her high-chair at the age of four. I shared her bedroom and the bed was piled high with feather mattresses. I thought I would try to stay awake until she came to bed as I was curious to see what her foot looked like without her boot. I never did find out, I was asleep long before she came into the room. The next day my Aunt took me to Whipsnade Zoo, I saw an elephant there who played the mouth organ on the end of its trunk. I then returned to Leighton Buzzard.

It was late August, the harvest was in full swing, and my Aunt took me to watch the men in the fields cut the corn with their scythes. The women tied the corn into stooks and stood them in bundles of three or four to remain in the field to dry. It took all day to harvest one field and the men and women only stopped for lunch and a drink, working on until dusk. It was fascinating to watch the rabbits as they ran nearer and nearer to the centre of the field, looking for somewhere to hide as their cover gradually diminished. Finally, the men shot the poor little things when there was nowhere left to run. We went to a cottage to deliver a rabbit and there was a lady doing her washing in a butler sink, she was rubbing the clothes on a wash board. I knew it was rude to stare but she only had one arm and I was fascinated.

3 September 1939
War is declared

At the beginning of September the family arrived to take me home, we sat at a wooden table in the garden eating porridge and I was pleased to note by the expressions on my siblings' faces that they thought the same as I did about the taste of salt instead of sugar on the oats. While we were there Mr Chamberlain, the Prime Minister, announced on the radio that England had declared war on Germany! I realised that this was serious by the expressions on the faces of the 'grown-ups' and the conversations they were having were so quiet that we children couldn't hear what was being said.

My Father's next posting was to Fort Brockhurst in

Gosport. The fort was a conundrum to me, from the outside it was like a huge hill but when I was inside I could see the sky.

    A disappointment for me while at Brockhurst was that Joy and David went to Elson village school, but there wasn't enough room for Gerald and myself. Once again I found I was looking through school railings instead of being inside; although I think it was harder this time as I'd already been to school and it was something I really enjoyed. Whilst at Brockhurst we saw a lot of my Grandmother Russell who lived in the town, and each Sunday we would meet her at the Bethel Mission for Sailors. Sometimes my Father would preach and if I was feeling tired I would snuggle up against my Mother. I can still feel her fur coat, so soft and warm. I often slept during the evening sermon! The main preacher was Mr Cook, he owned a grocery shop and sometimes after Sunday School we went to the Cooks' for tea. I found this quite an ordeal as he said we couldn't leave the table until our tummies touched the table, although I pulled my chair as close to the table as possible my tummy still wouldn't reach....

    My Father would take the four children for a walk on Sunday mornings. Our favourite route was over Rowner Bridge to see the aeroplanes at HMS Grange. This airfield was owned by the Fleet Air Arm and we would watch the planes take off and land. There was a wire fence surrounding the airfield, but we would push our noses against the fence to get the best view. I have a vague memory of seeing Flying Boats, but I think they must have been at Stokes Bay or Lee-on-the-Solent.

    When we had a day out to Southsea from Gosport we would go to the 'Hard' and get onto the car ferry. It cost a penny and made a loud clanking noise as it was pulled across the harbour on heavy chains. The car ferry took us to Old Portsmouth which was within walking distance of Southsea, while the passenger ferry berthed at Portsmouth Harbour, which was handier for shopping.

    I would like to mention the 'Mudlarks' in Portsmouth who were quite a tourist attraction though not really something of which the City could be proud. Children of all ages would wallow in the mud under the ferry pontoon, scrabbling to retrieve coins that people would toss down to them. They'd dig frantically in the mud with their bare hands searching for pennies; hence the name 'Mudlarks'. I believe this was made illegal sometime in the early fifties, as a high percentage of the children were suffering from TB (tuberculosis) in the bones.

    In 1940 my Father was again posted, this time to Larkhill on Salisbury Plain. We were in the first house of a long row of green detached 'Steel Houses', and the 'other Ranks' lived in the others, the Privates' families living at the far end of the row. The house was made of steel, hence the name. From the left of the front bedroom window we could see Stonehenge, and directly ahead what looked to me like a line of huge mole-hills which were old burial mounds called Barrows. The camp was half a mile down the road from the quarters, the

Gosport

HMS Grange

Southsea

Larkhill

Packway shops and local school were a mile across the fields. Behind the houses was a copse, more open fields and a river, it was wonderful and a huge improvement on the location of our previous quarters. The first day, we children must have driven my Mother mad. We ran round the house banging on the walls and thought the resounding noise was great fun, like living inside a giant drum, boom- boom- boom as we raced from room to room. It was the first time we had our own garden, at the front, side and back. What more could children ask for?

Walking to school across the field disturbed the many skylarks; they'd fly up from their nests, singing in annoyance at being disturbed and flying higher and higher until they were out of sight. There was an abundance of wild flowers, cowslips, buttercups, wild hyacinths and oxslips, and most days the teacher would be presented with a small nosegay gathered by the children on their way to school. Butterflies were in abundance and I particularly remember the delicate colour of 'The Chalk Blue' butterfly. I would look at the clouds and imagine I saw faces in them, I swear that one afternoon there was a Scotsman wearing a Tam-O'Shanter smiling down at me. In the winter however, when the snow lay thick on the ground or heavy rain-storms drove across the Plain, **School lorry** the Army would send a lorry to pick up the children and take them to school by road. After my first day in the lorry I learnt it was a better trip if you got in last rather than first… less suffocating! All the children had to take a chocolate bar or a packet of biscuits to be stored in a tin in the trenches. We were fitted for gas-masks, which we had to take everywhere with us. The under fives had a mask with a Mickey Mouse face on it, while babies had a large contraption in which they could sleep. We were all issued with Identity Cards, which had to be carried at all times. I think the number of the ID card stays in the memory the same way as a serviceman remembers his ID number.

The head mistress, Mrs Webb, always insisted we had a clean handkerchief when we arrived at school. One day I forgot mine and she sent me home to get one. The snow that day was particularly deep and seven year old legs are not very long, especially when the ditches were indiscernible from the flat ground. I lost count of the number of times I fell into the hidden ditches and lost my bearings. It must have taken me nearly two hours to get home as I didn't arrive until eleven a.m. and school started at nine a.m. I have never seen my Mother so angry as she was that day. She made me a cup of hot cocoa and sat me in front of the fire while she stormed off to school. No telephones in those days.

Incendiaries One night there was a huge fire at the Army camp. A number of troops had arrived the day before in transit to being posted abroad – they were all killed by the incendiary bombs. Next morning, as children do, we went into the woods searching for the empty incendiary cases. The smell of sulphur impregnated our clothes and it's a smell that's not easy to forget.

My Father only came home at weekends while we were at Larkhill, but when he did he would open his suitcase which he'd filled with his chocolate ration and saved for us.

Saturday night was hair night. My Mother would put a white cloth on her lap and after a 'Drene' shampoo, she'd go through our hair with a 'nit comb'. Afterwards she would twist my wet hair up with rags. While all this was going on my Father would sit on the back door-step and play his accordion. He was quite a good musician but Mother wouldn't allow him to play his music in the house.

Nits

Sundays were a ritual. Starting with breakfast in bed, we had a 'KitKat', 'Crunchy' and 'Milky Way', then it was into our best clothes and shoes for Morning Service. After dinner the children went to Sunday School. In the evening the whole family went to church. Before going to bed, we sat in a circle round the fire taking turns to read passages from the Bible. Although I was only seven years old I can't remember not being able to read, and the Bible isn't the easiest book in the world with its strange language and complicated names. Again this is a credit to the Army education system.

Sundays

The school wasn't quite sure what to do with us 'Silvers' at morning assembly as we were neither C of E nor RC, so each morning we would have to cross the road to the Salvation Army hall for morning prayers. I was forbidden to mix with the children from the other end of the quarters, which, of course made them more interesting. One day I went across the fields to the Packway with a girl from the other end of the quarters who was on an errand to the butcher to buy sausages. On the way home she started to eat them raw, telling me to try them as they were delicious. I did, they were, and I promptly threw up! I also remember going into her house and thinking it was much more interesting than ours … it was so untidy! There were children everywhere, boiling milk spilled over onto the black range and the Mother seemed so calm amongst all the mayhem. I was also persuaded to meet her in the afternoon with a penny … easy! I took it out of my Mother's purse. We went to the camp cinema. We sat right at the front on wooden chairs and the remainder of the audience was soldiers. It was very exciting. The stars were Jack Hulbert and Cicely Courtnidge in a film about a haunted Scottish Castle. When I arrived home I was in big trouble; (a) for stealing and (b) for going to the pictures. My Father punished me with his belt. From then on I stayed away from the children at the other end of the quarters.

We had several visitors during our stay at Larkhill. I have this strong recollection of my Uncle Ernie, standing in the back garden with his sailor's collar blowing in the wind. He was very handsome. He had been on HMS *Ark Royal* but luckily, (or so we thought at the time), he left the ship before it was sunk, though there were no casualties at that time as the crew was rescued by HMS *Legion* before the ship went down. It was the last time I saw him. He was killed when his next ship HMS *Beverly* was torpedoed by the German Navy.

We had a long visit from Aunt Ellen and my two cousins Bob and Brian. They stayed quite a while as they'd been bombed out of their house in Gosport. Sleeping arrangements were fun, albeit a bit crowded. We would sleep 'top to tail', that is:- girls at one end of the bed and the boys at the other … fine if everyone remembered to wash their feet before retiring! My Uncle Ben arrived at Christmas; he had found his family somewhere else to live on the outskirts of Gosport. Uncle Ben was a great favourite with children as his verses made us laugh, he usually recited his verses during dinner making the children double up with fits of laughter. One example I recall is:

> *The boy stood on the burning deck,*
> *His feet were covered in blisters,*
> *A cracker blew his trousers off,*
> *And he had to borrow his sister's.*

I cannot remember where my Father was posted to at this time, I think it was Chester, but we stayed at Larkhill. My Mother started to work at the NAAFI and Joy was left in charge of us in the evenings. She became very bossy! Then my Grandmother Russell came to stay. She had her own method of making us go to sleep at night instead of mucking about. It was called her slipper. She was a 'dab hand' at whacking us through the bedclothes, it didn't hurt, but we soon got the message and settled down to sleep. We each had our own chores to do. One would wash dishes, one would dry dishes, one would put polish on shoes and the other buffed them up, these chores were rotated each day.

July Bugs

There was great excitement one night in July; it had been hot and humid all day and when we went to bed there was this sound like stones falling down the chimney. Large 'cockroach' like insects came tumbling down in their hundreds (well, it seemed like hundreds to me!). My Mother rushed to get sheets of newspaper to cover over the fireplaces and we were kept awake as we listened to them falling into the grate. Next morning the paper was removed to reveal a pile of dead insects in the fireplace. Mother said they were called 'July Bugs,' a phenomenon of Salisbury Plain. (Does anybody know what they really were? They were similar to locusts.)

Bullying

There was a family a couple of doors away consisting of one girl my age and her four older brothers. They made my life hell with their bullying and name-calling. I would wait until they were halfway across the field before venturing out to school, I was so scared of them. One morning the girl was on her own, we were both late so we took a short cut under a barbed wire fence. I held it up while she went under and she held it up for me. When I was halfway through she let the wire go. It sprang into my back like a piece of elastic, cutting through my dress and into my skin. I stood up, my back stinging and saw that she was laughing; I slapped her face very hard. She ran to school crying and when I arrived some ten minutes later I was met by an angry head teacher who made me stand on a chair, with my back to the class, for an hour. I didn't think this was fair. The consolation was that the bullying stopped, so it was worth it. My Mother would make us recite 'Sticks and stones may break my bones, but names will never hurt me'. It didn't always work.

During my stay at Larkhill I was told by the other children how babies were made and taught alternative words to popular songs. 'After the ball was over' and 'In the shade of the old Apple Tree' are songs which even now I only know the 'dirty' version. I could not believe that my parents did the things I'd been told, so I asked my Mother where she'd got us from. She replied 'A special shop that sells babies for a pound each'. I liked this answer – it meant we must have been very rich to buy babies four times! It also made sense to me that the more children there were in a family, the scruffier they appeared, because the parents had spent all their money in the baby shop.

One summer's day we went for a picnic to Stonehenge and while we were there a terrible thunderstorm started (Salisbury Plain is not the best place to be when there's lightning about). A nearby farmer offered us shelter in his barn and asked us if we would like a drink. When we said 'yes' he went to the cow and drew off some milk. The taste was warm and wonderful. **Milk from the cow**

We would often walk up the lane towards the village of Amesbury, we'd follow the path along the side of the river until we came to a smallholding. The owner would allow us to pick as many sweet-peas as we could hold for sixpence. We'd take them home to Mother and their perfume filled the house for days.

The war was starting to affect our lives. We wrote a 'V' followed by three dots and a dash (Morse code for 'Victory') on the outside of the house and hated everything German, even German dogs! My Mother's first employer, Miss Kelly, came to stay with us for a while and I can remember the horror we felt when a swastika fell out of her purse. It was only the size of a small brooch, but we were convinced she was a spy. She didn't stay very long and my Mother could offer no explanation.

We were told we were going to America, we'd stay with relatives in California who owned an orange grove. This sounded wonderful to us, although I hadn't a clue where America was or how long it would take to get there, but it sounded as if it should be near Jamaica if oranges grew there. We went to Woolworth's (the threepenny and sixpenny store) where we each bought a small case. When we arrived home we were told to pack our favourite things to take on our journey. Mine contained mainly pencils and note-books, but I included my autograph book. My older brother had drawn an aeroplane and my younger brother had drawn a ship. Miss Kelly had written 'You're nearer God's heart in a garden, than anywhere else on earth'. I must have liked these words to remember them after so many years, but mostly it contained silly little verses written by friends at school, e.g. 'By hook or by crook I'll be last/first **'Going to America'** in this book'. I also packed a small, blue plastic bear that I'd bought, but no clothes! Our trip to America was cancelled abruptly. The Ellermen Line's ship 'City of Benares' left Liverpool on 13 September 1940 with ninety children on board, it was torpedoed by the Germans on 17 September and only thirteen children survived. Evacuating children by sea was now deemed to be too hazardous.

A car comes

One Sunday in September 1941, as we came over the hill from Sunday School we noticed a red car parked outside our gate. The sun was shining, it was one of those warm late summer days, everything in my world was perfect. 'Yes', I knew there was a war on, but it didn't affect me personally. Like the average eight year old, whatever the big wide world was up to I was only aware of my own family and immediate surroundings. I was blissfully unaware that this would be the last time I'd feel this happy, and that my whole world was about to be turned upside down. To us a car was a novelty, seeing it parked outside our gate made us curious enough to race home to find out what it was all about. In the front room were two middle-aged strangers, one male, one female and a golden cocker spaniel dog. I don't remember much about the woman, except that she had a Silver Fox fur draped around her shoulders, her steel-grey hair was pulled back from her face and curled in a sausage at the nape of her neck, when she smiled her teeth were brown, she wasn't very attractive. As to the man, I took to him instantly, he resembled the newspaper pictures of Winston Churchill, and everybody knew he was a good person. This man was of average height, quite stout, straight silver hair combed well back, his skin was very pale but he smiled all the time. The woman asked if my sister and I would like to go with them for a holiday. My mind thought, 'middle of school term, my small case upstairs packed for a journey, we were off to America where you could pick oranges off the trees'. We said 'yes' and excitedly climbed into the car (which was another first for us) not realising we'd started a journey which was to end our childhood. I was eight years old and my sister Joy was ten years old.

PART TWO

1940–50

WE TRAVELLED THROUGH THE VILLAGE OF AMESBURY TOWARDS Salisbury, through the City and north towards Wilton. The car turned right off the Wilton road and halfway up a hill came to a halt in the drive-way of a semi-detached house. I can't remember any conversations during the journey, except that we were to call them Auntie Marie and Uncle Percy and the dog was called 'Girlie'. We walked into the house via the kitchen door and into a dining-cum-sitting room. In each corner sat an old man. One was called Charlie Watts and the other one, who could have played Father Christmas without any make-up, was called Pop Bulford, his long beard was snowy white and his blue eyes gave us a friendly twinkle. A picture on the wall caught my attention, a small boy stood on a stool in front of a table, he was dressed in a pale blue velvet suit and was looking at a row of men sitting in front of him, underneath the picture was written 'When did you last see your Father?' I lost count of the number of times my eyes were drawn to that picture in the years that followed.

We didn't have bedrooms of our own. Joy was taken to a house opposite to sleep and I was shown how to make a bed on the landing out of a wardrobe. It was a strange contraption, there was a drawer at the bottom of the cabinet which contained sheets, pillows and blankets, there was a handle at the top, which, when pulled down a bed unfolded from the cupboard. From then on that was my space! I think excitement and fatigue must have taken over because I don't recall anything else about that first day.

Monday morning we were enrolled at the local school in Highbury Avenue, it seemed quite natural as we were old hands at changing schools. Our routine over the next couple of months was strange to say the least. We'd had enough of this so called holiday after a couple of weeks, and I wanted to return to my brothers and Mother. There were no oranges and we certainly weren't in America. We were taken into Salisbury to the Army and Navy tailors to be measured for new camel coats with tie belts. We were also taken to the hairdressers and 'treated' to an 'Eton crop'. This was supposed to be the most stylish hair-do of the day, the hair was cut very, very short and clippers were run up the back of the neck like a military short-back-and-sides. I wanted to die! I was so embarrassed I didn't want to go to school the next day with such a hairstyle.

Salisbury

'Auntie Marie and Uncle Percy'

Wardrobe bed

Highbury Avenue School

An 'Eton crop'

Chores before school

As the days turned into weeks we were gradually being taught what was expected of us. Out of our beds at six o'clock every morning, my first task was to strip my bed and put everything back in the drawer, then lift the handle to roll back the bed so it became a wardrobe once again. Joy had to clean and blacklead the fireplace in the backroom, dust and vacuum. I had to take the kitchen mat outside to be brushed on an old table in the garden, then scrub the floor which was made of red quarry tiles. I followed this by vacuuming the stairs and hall. When the chores were complete, I was to take a soft boiled egg, thin bread and butter and a cup of tea upstairs to Aunt Marie, (from now on I will call them Mr & Mrs L). Mr L was a diabetic, for his breakfast he had porridge followed by a slice of fried 'Hovis' bread and a fried egg. Sometimes he would do an extra piece of bread for me and I would spread marmalade on it, which I loved. Another breakfast I enjoyed was the new 'Dried Egg', it was sold in small packets and when mixed with water and brought to the boil it tasted like real scrambled eggs (well I thought so at the time). The saucepan was easier to clean as well! We then changed into our gymslips and went to school.

Chores after school

At lunch time we would come home for dinner, but first we had to wait on the adults sitting at the table. We would eat our dinner on the wooden table in the kitchen, doing the washing up before returning to school. In the evenings there were the bedrooms to be cleaned and after tea vegetables were to be prepared for the following day's meals. My sister and I were not allowed to talk if we were in the same room, but mostly we were kept to different parts of the house. I finally went to bed at eleven p.m. Strangely though, I was jealous of Joy because the people in whose house she slept were very kind to her. My only pleasure was the 'chore' I was given of walking the dog, the freedom of actually leaving the house. The route I had to take was across the allotments in Devizes Road and it had been timed to take one hour exactly. I found a tree I could climb and I'd sit in the branches hidden from passers by. Girlie would sit at the bottom while I could see and hear every one who passed. I would take every possible opportunity to read. *Grimms' Fairy Tales. Kelpie*, *John Halifax, Gentlemen* and *The Seven Pillars of Wisdom* were books I read. Mr L bought me an illustrated book about Pompeii and another with beautiful photographs of Norway. I became very adept at reading under the bedclothes with a torch. An advantage of sleeping on the landing was that I could always hear when someone was about to come up the stairs.

After several months (which seemed like several years to me) and still no sign of family, we had to take notes to school to say we would be absent the next day. We were dressed in our best clothes, new shoes, coats and dresses and taken by car to Salisbury Guildhall. We sat on a polished bench facing two very large, solid wooden doors, in an area so vast that the slightest whisper made an echo. The main door opened and Mother walked through, 'Hooray we were going home' was my immediate thought ... but something was wrong, she went through the doors opposite without saying a word. My Father came through the main door, gave us a hug and went through the same doors my Mother had gone through, Mr & Mrs L then followed them. After what seemed a very long time, our parents came out, said 'goodbye' and left. Then Mr & Mrs L came out and we followed them back to the car. I was feeling very unhappy and confused and wondered why my parents had gone again without taking us home. I wanted to go back with the family, I was missing my brothers and although my sister and I shared the same house, we were never allowed to be together. It was most distressing and painful. On the way back to their house Mrs L said, 'Your names are now Limpert not Silver and you call us Mummy and Daddy. I tried to have you named Gillian instead of Joan but it wasn't allowed.' After dinner we went back to school. Our names had already been changed on the register. Joy and Joan Silver no longer existed, instead we were these two new children that we didn't want to be, or were even asked if we wanted to be. Even our Identity Cards had been changed, but strangely the numbers were the same. To say I felt desolate would be an understatement, I was totally dazed and nothing seemed real. I would dream of my Mother sitting on a pedestal like an angel, then I would wake up crying. I really could not understand what was happening to me and the way my life was changing. It was 23 January 1942.

The school we went to had a large, silver barrage balloon in the playground, supposedly to protect us from German aircraft. We only had two scares with bombs, one hit a bridge and rattled all the windows, the other gave my sister and me much cause for laughter. Mrs L was in the garden when a German pilot started to fire his machine-gun at her, she screamed as she ran indoors and hid under the dining-room table. We had trenches at school where we would go as soon as the air raid siren wailed, always making sure we carried our gas-masks with us in case of a gas attack. Once there we would play 'Chinese whispers'. These always caused a laugh as the message at the end of the line bore no resemblance to the original whisper; and we'd sing songs such as 'Roll out the Barrel', 'Pack-up your troubles in your old kit bag', 'Kiss me Good-night Sergeant Major' and 'Ten Green Bottles' (not exactly like the pop songs of today). We sat on wooden benches and the dank smell was horrible. As soon as the 'All Clear' sounded we marched back to our classrooms to continue our lessons. I think I had a vivid imagination at this time, as I was often asked to go to one of the other classes at the end of the day to tell the children a story. I was never prepared, but somehow always managed to have a beginning, middle and end.

I had a boyfriend. We would write notes to each other and place them under a loose brick on the outside of the air-raid shelter on the way home. It was comforting to know that at least one person liked me. Girl friends were more difficult. If I was asked to go to their homes to play, or to their birthday parties, I had to decline as permission was always refused. They thought I didn't want to be friends, which of course was far from the truth. At the end of my first

Change of name

23 January 1942

Air raid siren

Highbury junior school

term in the new school I took home my first school report. We didn't know the contents as they were always in sealed envelopes, they had to be signed by the parents before being returned to the school at the beginning of the next term. I wasn't unduly worried as I had come third in a class of over forty children. I was caned at the back of my legs for not coming top. Mind you, the next year in the top class I came second. Another hiding. You can imagine what happened when at the end of the last term of junior school I came twelfth! I would never be top of the class, there was a boy who always did, and I knew I couldn't beat him.

Mr Ayres

Mr Ayres taught the top class at Highbury junior school, he controlled his class of forty plus pupils strictly but fairly. We sat at our desks in straight rows, the high achievers at the front and the less skilled at the back. This may seem strange, but his desk was on a small platform and meant he had a clearer view of the pupils at the back of the room. By the side of his desk he had a large hamper full of canes, all different widths, but I never once saw him cane a child, just reaching for the lid of the hamper brought instant silence and attention. He had such a high percentage of pupils passing the 'Eleven Plus' that the powers that be gave us an extra half day holiday. While I was in his class I volunteered to be the 'cod liver oil' monitor. The rule was that every morning, each child be given

Monitor

a spoonful of this nauseating liquid. The advantage of being monitor was that I poured it down everybody else's throat, washed the spoons afterwards but never took a dose myself. The government also decreed that children have a third of a pint of milk each day, completely free. The crates would be delivered to the playground and in the winter months it was most enjoyable, very cold and refreshing, but in the warmer weather it tasted awful, verging on the 'about to turn sour'. It was not unusual to have two bottles to drink most days, as some of the children didn't like milk, but I did and drank the spares so to speak. The other monitor's job I had was to stand at the door after I'd rung the handbell in the playground and take down the names of the late-comers as they arrived. I really enjoyed my days at Highbury Avenue School.

I feel I owe Mr Ayres an apology after reading my efforts at writing this book. The first day in his class he wrote 'nice' 'get' and 'got' on a piece of paper, screwed it up and threw it into the waste-paper basket. He said we were never to use those three words in written compositions as the English language had many better words to describe what we meant. I feel I've let him down several times … sorry, Sir!

Sweet shop

Opposite the school was a small shop, which before the war did brisk business selling sweets to the school children. This all stopped when sweet rationing was introduced, but we could buy 'one penny' bottles of drink (they were really just bottles of coloured, sweetened water) and the girls soon discovered that if they drank the red drink it stained their lips and looked as if they were wearing lipstick. During my time at junior school we'd go on nature walks to the meadows, where we learnt first hand the shapes and names of leaves from the various trees, watch the dragon-flies flitting across the water, the minnows and other pond life. I can remember the sweet taste from the flower head of clover and understanding why the bees loved clover so much. We collected frog-spawn in a jam-jar and took them home hoping to see them develop into frogs, but I was never successful, I think the sun shining on the kitchen window must have semi-cooked them as they always died prematurely. I still believe, though, that learning 'in the field' so to speak is a much better way to learn than reading books or watching television.

We'd start each day stripped to our knickers and vest (for decorum, boys were allowed to keep on their short-legged, grey flannel trousers) for exercises in the playground. We'd jump up and down moving our arms and legs in a sort of scissor routine, arms stretch, knees bend, touch our toes and up again. I can assure you that on a cold frosty morning it was a good way to get the circulation going, a perfect way to clear one's head for the day's lessons ahead. **Physical jerks**

The sexes were separated at playtime each having their own play area. Skipping was the main game for girls and we would have competitions over who could do the most 'bumps (double the turns of the rope per jump)' I think the record at the time was forty-four. We would chant 'Mrs D - Mrs I- Mrs FFI- Mrs C- Mrs U- Mrs LTY', a brilliant way to learn spelling. The other popular one was 'Mrs M- Mrs I- Mrs SSI- Mrs S- Mrs I- Mrs PPI'. Another playground game was 'Five stones' a favourite of mine as I had the advantage of large hands. Hopscotch was also very popular; drawing the squares and writing the numbers in chalk on the playground, we then threw a stone to the numbers in numerical order and had to hop to the appropriate square. Handstands and cartwheels could become very competitive, yet none of these games cost money so everyone was on an equal footing so to speak. **Skipping**

I would like to mention some of the people who made life a little more bearable, every kind word or small act of kindness was something to treasure and hold on to. The lady next door was crippled with arthritis, but gave us beautiful hand made presents at Christmas. An old lady lived two doors away and she made the most delicious Caraway seed cakes. She would bring them to the door in a tin and say she had made too much and would we help her by eating it up; and at Christmas she would bring us her home made sultana wine in large stone-ware jars.

When I was about ten years old I went for a holiday to the village Post Office at Farley. The owners were friends of Mr L and had an only son. It was thought I would make a playmate for him during the school holiday. He had a room that was completely filled with toys … a child's Aladdin's Cave. We played together very happily as he was pleased to have company whilst his parents worked in the shop. We went for walks in the local woods, where there were so many bluebells you couldn't find a space to walk without treading on them, the colour blue stretched as far as the eye could see. It was a truly wonderful sight and aptly named 'Bluebell Wood'. On Sunday we helped the Vicar of the village **A good friend at Farley** church to pump the organ, for which he paid us threepence each, I think we would have done it for free as it was more fun than sitting in the pews and listening to his sermon! One Sunday my new friend didn't want to go to Matins, so we stayed at home by ourselves while the grown ups went to the Service. We decided to play at 'grown-ups' and climbed into his parents bed, sitting up and pretending to drink tea. He gave me a ring (which must have cost at least sixpence in Woolworth's) and decided we were now engaged. I don't know why these visits suddenly stopped as I was truly happy when I stayed at Farley. The ring? … Mr L cut it off when my finger started to turn green!

Aunt May

I feel that I must dedicate a whole section to Aunt May, as she was a great influence in my life and a cushion during my formative years with the Ls, a bolt-hole of sanity perhaps is the best way of describing my brief visits to her home.

One day we went by car to Blandford Forum in Dorset to fetch Mr L's Mother. She was born in the Dorset village of Moor Critchel in the mid-eighteen hundreds, she'd married a farm labourer, raised two children and never travelled any further afield. I believe the longest journey she ever took was to Southampton Hospital where she had treatment for cancer when she was well into her sixties. She'd taken lodgings above a shoe shop in Blandford after her husband died, as she was unable to remain in the tied farm cottage that had been her home throughout her marriage. We stopped outside a shop by the name of L. Teare and were greeted by a little Lancashire lady who told us to call her Aunt May. I can still remember the fantastic smell of leather as I walked through the shop door … wonderful. The house itself was a maze of staircases, two Georgian houses had been made into one and there were stairs and doors everywhere. It was an absolute joy for children to go up a flight of stairs at the front of the house, through a maze of corridors and doors, and emerge at the back of the work-room. At the back of the house was an alleyway which led to the river Stour. There were mystery noises coming from the top of the house, and I learnt afterwards that Aunt May's husband, Louis, was bed ridden and an alcoholic. It was explained to me that his drinking was to alleviate the pain from a metal plate in his leg and another in his head. He had been badly wounded during the First World War, in which he served as an army officer. Aunt May met him when she was a nurse in a military hospital. He had the trade of surgical boot maker and taught his wife all he knew. They had no children and I found out much later that at one time she'd wanted to adopt me from the Ls … If only!

Blandford

Some time after our initial meeting, Aunt May asked if I could stay for a week's holiday. I boarded the bus at Salisbury Bus Station and travelled the twenty-two miles to Blandford. It took about an hour and the driver would stop every-so-often to drop off a parcel at a lonely cottage or farm gate. Quite a crowd of Gypsies would use the bus after a day hawking their pegs and lucky heather sprays round the City, but they only travelled about ten miles before coming to their caravan site. Aunt May's was a different world. I would get breakfast in bed, bacon, eggs and field mushrooms freshly picked by one of her employees at four o'clock that morning. My bedroom was on the third floor, and the bed was pure luxury – feather mattresses and white linen sheets. It was sparsely decorated, the walls were distempered white, but on the wall was a set of cartoon prints of 'Old Bill' in the trenches; the only furniture was a wash-stand and basin and I hung my clothes from the picture-rail. Under the bed was a large chamber-pot. There was no bathroom or any other 'mod-con'. Visiting Aunt May was an oasis of calm to me yet she was strict and I had to earn my keep by dusting, washing up and helping in the shop, but she was always fair and this I respected.

Uncle Louis had died and Aunt May was being courted by a soldier in the Hampshire Regiment. I called him Uncle Bert. He was very handsome and reminded me of Clark Gable with his neatly clipped moustache. One evening he took us to the Boscombe Hippodrome. We saw Jack Warner who came on stage pushing his bicycle, and using his catch-phrase 'Mind my bike'. 'Jane' of the *Daily Mirror* was also on the bill; she was considered very 'risqué' for those days as she appeared in the nude. She wasn't allowed to move when the curtain rose because the law didn't allow nudes to move on stage, so it was a series of poses i.e. 'girl on a swing' or 'girl with an umbrella', etc.

Aunt May's shop would be stacked with black army boots from floor to ceil-ing at the beginning of each week. You could hardly open the door there were so many. She had men working non-stop to repair the boots before the next consignment arrived. The American soldiers were now stationed at Blandford Camp and my Aunt had the Army contract. She worked very long hours and always seemed to be covered in black dust, some nights she would stay up until the early hours hand-stitching a pair of shoes or a pair of riding boots; her hands were hard and rough from the threads she used. She was no pushover where I was concerned, but she was always very fair and although I had a lot of chores to do I felt no resentment towards her. I realised that her life was harrowing with the long hours and a staff of men relying on her success. She would take me to Bournemouth where she bought her leather, which was becoming increasingly scarce and difficult to obtain, but she always managed to find enough to mend my shoes.

She lived in the three stories above the shop. In the front sitting-room she had an old radiogram, not many records though, but I liked to play Ronny Ronalde's *In a Persian Garden* and *Bells Across the Meadow*. One day while I was playing records I looked out of the window to see the whole street was a long convoy of lorries filled with Canadian Airmen going to war. I always thought the blue of their uniforms more attractive than the pale grey-blue colour of the RAF. When they saw me at the window they started to throw up bars of choco-late and packets of chewing gum. It endeared me to the Canadians for ever.

In the spring of 1945 I again went to Aunt May's for a holiday and while I was there she had a telegram to say her Aunt in Morecambe had died. We

VE Day

caught the train to Lancashire. We'd only been there a few days when it was announced on the radio that Germany had unconditionally surrendered to the Allies. It was the eighth of May and called 'VE Day.' (Victory Europe). All the fighting was now to be concentrated against the Japanese in Asia. Most people in my age group have memories of street parties, but I don't. Aunt May took me to the theatre at Morecambe Winter Gardens where we saw a musical called *The Maid of the Mountains*. I found the plot very confusing for a twelve year old. One thing that amused me about Aunt May was the fact that whenever Gracie Fields started singing on the radio she would cringe and mimic her high notes before turning the radio off. She never did explain why, but I think it was a bit of Lancastrian envy! When we returned to Blandford the stocks of boots were piling up, despite the fact that four men were working non-stop and a lady called Jessie served in the shop. My aunt sat on her three legged stool in front of the black range, hand stitching shoes till the early hours trying to catch up with the work

There was no running hot water in the Georgian property, no bathroom either and the exposed electric flexes would swing across the ceiling from one room to the other. There were however two toilets, one at the bottom of the stairs for the workmen and one upstairs next to the kitchen sink for us to use. Cooking was also fraught with problems. There was the black range, which permanently had a kettle of water boiling on it and non-electric irons keeping hot. The success of the food cooked in the oven never ceased to amaze me (there were no thermostats) but she made a wicked Lancashire Hotpot, succulent scones and a Victoria Sponge to die for (I think there was a barter system during the war for eggs and butter). This method of cooking was fine in the winter but the range was too hot to keep going in the summer; there was not a lot of ventilation from the small window at the back of the house, and when the front window was opened the noise and dust from the convoys filled

Paraffin cooker

the room. Aunt May had a paraffin cooker. It was a large, green square 'monster', standing against the wall of the dining room. I never worked out how it operated, but it must have been a hell of a fire hazard. Cardboard was placed under its front feet to keep it balanced as all the wooden floors were at an angle, in fact there wasn't a straight floor in the whole house. For lighting

Oil lamps and chamber pots

upstairs we used oil lamps and under each bed was a large chamber pot (a gozunder). One night, in 'mid pee' it split clean in two. I thought I would get a hiding for that, but Aunt May said 'Accidents happen', and that was the end of it.

Bath night

Bath night, a weekly event in those days, was an adventure. The zinc bath, that normally hung on the wall in the backyard, was carried upstairs by one of the workmen. Everything that could hold water, i.e. saucepans, kettles, metal jugs, etc. was heated up on the range. (good job we didn't have plastic buckets in those days). This method of heating water was more relaxing than the gas geyser at home which petrified me. Light the pilot light, turn on the water and then turn the pilot light on to ignite the gas and wait for the sound of a small explosion … s-c-a-r-e-y!) Here I could sit in front of the warm range and soak to my heart's content … heavenly. I even had the water topped up by Aunt May when it started to cool down, making bath-night a long lingering pleasure.

Aunt May had a golden cocker spaniel called 'Shammy'. She was younger than 'Girlie' and loved to go for walks. I only had to go the length of the main street and round the corner to be beside the river Stour. I'd stroll along the river bank and watch the men trying to catch fish. I can't honestly remember seeing a successful catch. I assume it's the anticipation that drives fishermen to stare at the water for hours on end and then return home and say 'It was a good day on the river today'! Sometimes Aunt May would give me a bunch of flow- ers to take to Uncle Louis' grave in the village of Blandford St Mary. She also owned a cottage in the village, she'd bought it for one of her workmen who'd escaped from the Channel Islands with his family during the German occupa- tion. These were halcyon days, even though there was still a war on. Children are very resilient to turmoil in the rest of the world, it's only their own imme- diate surroundings that make the difference between happy and sad.

Blandford St Mary

One day I found a tabby kitten and begged Aunt May to let me keep it. She replied: 'If it rattles, it's a boy and you can keep it, if it doesn't rattle it's a girl and you can't keep it'.

I was totally confused when the whole workshop, Aunt May, Jessie and some customers doubled up with laughter as I held the kitten against my ear and gave it a thorough shake! The kitten stayed and grew into a very handsome Tabby Tom.

There was a lot of excitement however when Uncle Bert proposed to Aunt May. They were to be married when he returned to England from Holland (where he was still stationed) and got his demob. I was slightly miffed (and that's an understatement) as Joy was to be the bridesmaid. Coupons were still required for clothes, but Aunt May had managed to get enough pink velvet to make a long dress. On the day she looked as lovely as any bride should. Mr L was in charge of the wedding cake, but there was an awful row at the reception as he'd put a stork carrying a baby on the top of the cake instead of the cus- tomary bride and groom. The bride and groom were not amused … Sort of spoilt the day!

One day Aunt May took me with her to visit her new in-laws in Corfe Mullen. We spent a very pleasant day in the country and arranged to catch the last bus from Bournemouth. We would board it in Wimborne and I think it then went all the way to Salisbury. We were at the head of the queue so weren't unduly worried that it would be too crowded. There were a lot of American soldiers in Wimborne that night and at pub closing-time they seemed to pour out onto the streets. Much to our disgust they relieved themselves against the wall behind the bus-stop. Aunt May's remarks are not repeatable and she did her best to shield me from the sight. By the time the bus arrived there was a

Corfe Mullen

very long queue of soldiers waiting to return to Blandford Camp, but instead of a slow procession onto the bus they just surged forward pushing us out of the way. The bus left the stop with soldiers hanging off the platform and two females still waiting at the front of the queue! My Aunt had a temper and at this precise moment she was furious and worried about us getting back to Blandford. She went to the nearest phone box and dialled '999'. A police car arrived in a very short time and the driver told us to get in. It was the fastest journey ever between Wimborne and Blandford. ... and we arrived before the bus!

I think it should be mentioned how I became addicted to the wicked weed tobacco. Watching films from Hollywood and being a particular fan of Bette Davis and Humphrey Bogart, not to mention Marlene Dietrich, smoking seemed the height of sophistication and the grown-up thing to do. On one of my visits to Aunt May, she and Uncle Bert took me to a dance in the Sergeant's Mess at Blandford Camp. I was fourteen years old at the time but still managed to spend the evening dancing with one of the soldiers (he was very old at eighteen). When the interval for refreshments arrived, we went outside to get some fresh air and he offered me a cigarette. Naturally I didn't want him to know how young I was, so I accepted. After a couple of puffs I had a very soggy Woodbine and a mouth full of tobacco. I asked him for another, he thought I was a chain smoker but I believed in 'practice makes perfect'. I'd started my slide down the slippery slope of bad habits.

Smoking

Cigarettes were very cheap to buy in the 1940s and some of the brands I remember are Woodbines, Players Weights and Park Drive. If I wanted to be posh and show off I'd buy Du Maurier, they were packed like a cigarette-case and seemed very feminine. Craven-A had a black cat on the packet; Passing Clouds, in their pale pink packet contained squashed cigarettes which looked as if some-one had sat on them by mistake. I must not forget the awful Nosegay cigarettes, these were very cheap and could be bought in a packet of five at a time. If you forgot to puff or put them down on the ashtray, they would go out and you'd have to relight them. Lastly the American Philip Morris and Camel brands, if you could drag on one of those and not cough you were truly a seasoned smoker!

Grandma L was a tiny little woman who was born in the 1850s, she wore her soft white hair neatly twisted into a bun on the top of her head. She always wore a white starched blouse buttoned to the neck and a black taffeta skirt to her ankles. She had a waist line to die for and I'm sure I could use one hand to encircle it. Her shoes were small black ankle boots tightly laced and highly polished. Mr L was her only son. He left the village school when he was twelve years old, the teachers said he had reached the required standard of Maths and English and they were unable to teach him further. There was no opportunity to go to Grammar School in those days if your father was a farm labourer earning 5/- a week! There was also a daughter called Margaret, she was a spinster in her mid-forties and worked as a house-maid in a large house in Salisbury. As

Aunt May now had the contract to repair the Army boots from the nearby camp she could no longer find the time to look after Granny L, so the Ls decided to take her to Salisbury. She was to lodge in the front room of a neighbour a few doors up the road from us called Pat Atkins. She had a young son and a husband who was a Major serving abroad for the duration of the war. This arrangement turned out in my favour as I would often visit Gran L with food and her clean laundry. Pat and I would spend time in the evenings playing cards; she taught me 'Knock Out Whist' and how to play draughts. It became a little haven away from the chores. When I was thirteen years old the front room became vacant at the L's and Granny L left Pat's and came to stay with us. Strangely enough she became an ally, as she disliked Mrs L as much as we did. She told us 'her son only married Molly on the rebound', I think she called her Molly to annoy her as she preferred to be known as Marie, thinking that Molly sounded common. She was a very knowledgeable old lady and said her hair was soft because she had always rinsed it in an infusion of Rosemary water. One of the many things she taught me was how to skin a rabbit, which I thought would be most useful if I ever had a family of my own ... but I must admit that fifty years on I've never had to do it! She thought the tastiest part of the rabbit was the brains. She would take a hair-pin to scoop it out and eat it with such relish you'd think it was Caviar to see the look of sheer enjoyment on her face. Not that I ever fancied it myself! If tea was accidentally spilled on the white linen table-cloth she would boil a kettle of water, place the stain over a basin and pour the water from the outside of the stain going round and round in circles, it gradually got smaller and smaller until it finally disappeared. One day while Mrs L was out, a rat shot through the back door, up the hall and into the front sitting-room. Granny L, all four foot nothing of her, told us to stand outside the door while she went in with her walking stick. Quite a lot of noise came from inside the room and when the door finally opened, Granny L was holding the dead rat by the tail. She said they were only dangerous if cornered. She got a hammer and a nail and pinned it onto the back door. We then waited for Mrs L to come home. When we heard the terrible scream, we fell about laughing.

I'd like to put on record some of the things about Granny L that were country lore, and are now lost in the mists of time. I mentioned before that she was Dorset born and bred, a lady whose life was hard with neither money nor possessions. Her knowledge though, was outstanding. When the man came to the door selling logs she would decimate his stock. She knew from which tree each log had come, which would give a good flame and which would fill the room with smoke. If she said the wood was too green. ... no sale. She was also excellent at reading the weather signs. As I grew older I relied on her a great deal for my dates in the evenings; the slightest hint of rain and Mrs L's permission to go out was withdrawn. To quote Gran, 'Rain before seven, fine by eleven' but if it was still raining at noon she would then quote: 'Rain before eleven, fine by seven'. Either way it gave one hope. 'Red sky at night, Shepherds delight' or

Granny L

Stain removal

Country lore

A kind old lady

'Red sky in the morning, Shepherds warning' were two more of her sayings which seem to be accurate to this day. If there was a small patch of blue in the cloudy sky she would say it was enough to make a pair of sailor's trousers, and would soon be fine again.

I now had a camp-bed (a folding bed made of light wood and canvas) which was most uncomfortable and I shared the front room with Granny L. As she dressed in the morning or undressed at night, I couldn't help thinking that I was not looking forward to growing up and wearing the tight laced corsets that women wore; I even had to pull Mrs L's laces tighter some mornings so that her dress or skirt would be a tighter fit. It was during this time that I learnt about her medical history. She had a circle of scars on her arm from Radium needles inserted around her skin cancer. Her left breast was missing, it had been cut away to the bone to cure breast cancer. She would cut a strip of orange 'Thermogene' cotton wool and lay it across the scar to keep it warm as the skin was so thin it barely covered the bone. She was in her mid-eighties during the war and the skin and breast cancer were treated at Southampton General Hospital sometime during the 1930s. It is to their credit and the skill of the surgical and nursing care at the time, that she suffered no recurrence of the disease. Hence I never thought of cancer as the death sentence it seems to be today.

After the affair with the rat Granny told me this story, but I can't prove or disprove its authenticity. Years before in her village, there was a mother feeding her new-born baby when a rat leapt onto the bed. It started to feed from her spare nipple. She was so frightened the rat might bite her or the baby that she just froze until the rat had finished. Very scary! Another of her tales concerned the bees. It appears that if someone dies in the family, the bees become very agitated in the hive and the only way to settle them again is to tell them who has died. She also said that you should never call anyone a dirty pig, as pigs are the cleanest animals on the farm and can't bear to be dirty.

Another reason for sharing the room with Granny L was that she now had a heart problem. If she awoke in the night unable to get her breath, I would break a small chalky phial under her nose and this would quickly revive her. Towards the end though, she became very weak and had a terrible bed-sore. It looked as if it had eaten away the flesh at the base of her spine, it was a deep hole and must have caused her agony. I was sad when she died, she had been a great ally against Mrs L.

A kind couple

I would like to mention a couple who were very kind to me called Mr and Mrs Wilson. They had no children of their own and I don't know how they came into contact with the L's. Pop Bulford had died and was lying in his open coffin in the front bedroom. His door was opposite the landing where I slept. Mrs L constantly came up with reasons for me to go into the bedroom. I was scared. I had never seen a dead body before and there was a sickly smell which seemed to permeate through the whole of the house. Maybe it was from the lilies laid on his chest. It was arranged that at seven o'clock each evening I was to go up the road, round the corner and into the Wilson's front gate. While there I had my own bedroom and was treated with untold love and kindness. It was a very different world. They would take me to the Salisbury Playhouse where we watched anything from Variety to Shakespeare. I particularly enjoyed Agatha Christie's 'Ten Little Nigger Boys' and the couple who sang duets from the films of Jeanette McDonald and Nelson Eddy. One evening I wanted to go to a social at the local Church Youth Club, permission of course was denied. When I arrived at the Wilson's there was an evening gown laid out on my bed for me to wear, it was a very pretty floral material and fitted me perfectly. I went to the social and had a wonderful time with other youngsters of my own age. Just as I was getting used to being spoilt it came to a sudden end. I never saw the Wilsons again. It was back to the bed on the landing and the late night chores.

Lodgers

There should have been space for me to have a room of my own now Pop had died, but we had Test Pilots from Boscombe Down, Polish Airmen and a string of other lodgers coming and going all the time. The Test-Pilots didn't stay long, they would breeze in and out like a breath of fresh air, they were noisy and full of fun, maybe it was the uncertainty of their job that made them behave as if there was no tomorrow. They always seemed to be laughing as if they hadn't a care in the world. The Polish lodgers were the opposite, very quiet and subdued. It was never safe for me to be alone with the younger men when I was cleaning their rooms though; they would creep up and grab me from behind, spin me round and try to kiss me. If they had been allowed and Mrs L had caught us, guess who would get the blame and ensuing punishment. One of the Poles was an older man and he soon put the younger ones in their place. He acted as a sort of father figure to the others. He showed me photos of his wife and children back in Poland. He hadn't heard from them since he'd left his country to join the Airforce. I hope they were reunited after the war. The sitting room downstairs also had a bed in it. Granny L had died and I, of course was back on the landing. It was now let to a lady called Kathleen. One morning Mrs L was beating me with the Hoover hose and Kathleen snatched it out of her hands. 'Don't do that again or I'll report you to the authorities,' she said. She was given notice to leave.

'Crimes'

Joy and I came to the same conclusion . . . Mrs L was a lunatic. She seemed to go completely mad whenever there was a full moon. We would be getting on with our chores when 'out of the blue' Mrs L would start laying into us with whatever came to hand. Sometimes a cane, a carpet beater or just her hand to your head and send you flying across the room. The 'crimes' we were punished for were so trivial – if we said 'What' instead of 'Pardon', maybe 'A?' Unforgivable and swiftly hit. I knew the pitfalls but when you're young the mouth tends to work before the brain is in gear, I seemed to fall into every trap no matter how hard I tried to have a trouble-free day. She never beat the two of us at the same time, it seemed one was in favour and the other out of favour. We were not allowed to talk or have any contact with each other, our chores sending us to different rooms in the house. It seems incredible looking back, that although we were sisters living in the same house neither one of us knew what the other was doing or suffering. We had no toys or personal possessions, we were not allowed to go out to play or mix with other children, the only contact with our own age group was at school. We spent a lot of time off school. Notes were sent saying we had colds, sore throats or ear infections, etc., the truth being that we were badly bruised or marked and Mrs L was afraid it would be seen when we changed for PT. Mr Bragger, the NSPCC man, would call to check that we were being looked after properly. He always gave warning of his visit and we would be dressed in our tailor made best clothes, the table would be well laid with food and everything cleaned and polished to perfection (by my sister and myself I might add). We were never left in the room on our own with Mr Bragger, when all he had to do was look at our shoulders and backs to see what was really going on, or ask to speak to us without 'her' being present. We badly needed an ally, but it was a time of 'Children should be seen and not heard', as if being young in years gave you no rights. One day Mrs L did get a shock, her precious cocker spaniel bit her while she was beating me. That dog was my best friend for life!

The NSPCC

It was difficult to know where we stood as people. We would have the best clothes money and coupons could buy, they were either made by a tailor or a dressmaker, we never left home without wearing our gloves, stockings and a hat. Food was plentiful in spite of rationing, so outside the house we were well cared for little ladies. Mrs L would be complimented on how well she dressed us, how we were a credit to her and weren't we lucky little girls to have such a good home with people who cared for us. As soon as we entered the back door it was a complete change-around, we had to take off our clothes and put on an overall (this was similar to a sleeveless cotton dress, with tapes tied round the waist). Now we were servants and skivvies, with no rights or status at all, and completely at the mercy of Mrs L's moods and tempers. It was a Jeckyll and Hyde existence which was most confusing to two young girls.

'Such a good home'

Bournemouth

I had one more experience with bombs. I was staying with a lady I called Aunt Olive who lived in a flat in Charminster Road, Bournemouth (I haven't a clue who she was, I only met her this once). Also staying at this time was her daughter with a new baby and four year old son. The second night of my stay the sirens went and the blast from a bomb threw me out of bed ... a very rude awakening! Aunt O's husband wouldn't stay in the flat with the women and children, but would pop in after every explosion and tell us what had been hit and where the fires were. Aunt O was looking after the four year old and told her daughter to hold the baby, then if they were buried in the rubble she would be able to breast feed him and keep him alive until they were rescued. At nine years old I was very scared and everyone seemed to have forgotten about me. I went to the toilet and promptly 'threw up'. I was very relieved to hear the 'all clear'. Next morning I took the baby and toddler out for a walk in the pram. Ten minutes after leaving the flat the 'siren' wailed, the front door of a house opened and a kindly lady invited us to come indoors until the 'all clear' sounded. Before we left, this thoughtful lady went into her garden to pick Victoria plums from the tree for us to take home. I was very grateful to that lady and I now realised that War was a serious business and not something that was happening miles away in another country.

Mr L would take me to 'Beales of Bournemouth' (a large department store) where we would sit in the upstairs restaurant and order a dinner of chicken and two veg, it cost five shillings, food was still rationed so it was quite a treat. When we managed to find a window seat we could look out over the Winter Gardens and the sea beyond, but what I really enjoyed were the fashion shows. The tall and elegant mannequins would glide gracefully between the tables as if they had all the time in the world, standing at each table in turn for the diners to admire the clothes they were modelling, clothes that were actually wearable. Very different to today's models who bounce down the cat walk, always in a hurry and wearing clothes that could get you arrested if you wore them in the street. The other reason he took me to Bournemouth was to visit the stamp shop, where he would buy additions for the collection my Father had started for me.

Another outing that stays in the mind was when we went to the village of Hythe in the New Forest, to visit an elderly relative of Mrs L's. It was a picturesque cottage deep in the forest, with a stream running alongside the front garden. The water was so clear the tramps would drink from the ditch, it also fed a well in the garden and was as cold and clear as a mountain stream. The garden itself was well stocked with fruit trees and fresh vegetables. The old lady was in her nineties and showed us some of the tapestries she'd made. I marvelled at the agility of such an elderly lady, but the best part was the dinner. We had jugged hare. The flavour of the black gravy was a taste I had never experienced before, or since, it was absolutely delicious! I've been told that the hare has to hang until it crawls with maggots before it's cooked. I was unaware of that at the time, but perhaps that's why I haven't searched too hard for a recipe.

Hythe

I would just like to add to the subject of Mrs L and our daily routines. Although the beatings were frequent, in between there was the gradual erosion of any self esteem. No matter how hard we tried, nothing was good enough. We were continually reminded that our parents didn't want us, that we were ugly and if we didn't do as we were told we would be sent to a remand home. I didn't know what that meant, but the tone of the threat translated in my mind that it must be worse than the present situation. The trouble with me was that when I was in pain I would yell and cry, whereas Joy would suffer in silence. She'd bite her bottom lip until it bled rather than make a sound. There was one instance that I remember very clearly. Joy was cleaning the hearth on her knees and bent forward. I was brushing down the stairs and thinking how lucky my

Beatings

sister was to have such nice hair, it was chestnut brown and waved gently down her back, unlike mine which was mousy and dead straight. Suddenly Mrs L appeared and started beating Joy across the shoulders. She didn't make a sound. I screamed, 'Leave her alone, leave her alone'.

What happened next I don't remember. I was worried about my sister as she was becoming very pale and thin. There was so much TB among young girls in their teens but I think it was just her unhappiness making her lose weight.

Kindness to animals

Although Mrs L thought nothing of abusing two young girls, she was extremely kind to animals and lost causes. The latter I will explain. There was an Italian with a large black moustache called 'Benny', he would stand in the road with a 'Hurdy Gurdy' on a pole and as he turned the handle a monkey would jump up and down to the music. Mrs L always invited him indoors to give him a hot meal and drink and sometimes gave him half a crown before sending him on his way. There was also an old tramp who called once a year. Looking back I think he must have been suffering from Parkinson's Disease, his hands would shake so much he couldn't drink his tea, Mrs L would pour it into a saucer and hold it to his mouth so that he could drink without spilling it down the front of his ragged old coat. The irony of these two old down-and-outs being brought into the house was that they were allowed to sit in the dining-room . . . with Joy or me waiting on table! Mrs L. told me that they once lived in the New Forest and if you were kind to a tramp he would mark your gate with a chalk cross so that other tramps would know they would be welcome.

One day Mr L heard some strange noises in the garden coming from his cab-bages. When he looked to see what it was there were three very wet and very young kittens. They certainly knew how to make themselves heard, their eyes were still closed and they were too young to leave their mother. He moved them into the garage where they would be warm and dry, placed them on an old blanket and put some milk and food down for their mother. The next day they were back in the rain among the cabbages, so Mr L brought them indoors to sit in the hearth by the coal fire. After they'd dried out and were tired of spit-ting at us, which was quite funny as they were so small and helpless, they were put in a box. Girlie decided to mother them and she took on the chore of con-tinuously licking them. The 'she' kitten was put down (no spaying for queens in those days) and the black kitten attached itself to Joy. The long haired tabby, who grew to be the size of a Jack Russell dog, became my pet. At night he would creep under my bed clothes and curl up on my feet, not making a sound when Mrs L kept calling to put him out for the night. I would wear woollen bed-socks in bed (okay, it was cold on the landing and there was no central heating) and 'Fluffy' would make the wool soaking wet with his dribbling and kneading. As it was war time, fish was hard to obtain. Every Saturday I had to go into town to queue for some cod or whichever fish was available, this was then boiled up for the cats. Even now I don't like the smell of fish. It seems incredible, but the fish had to be skinned and filleted before being cooked, only the best for the pets. It was useful … I learnt to fillet fish! like skinning a rabbit no good to me at all, but they say knowledge is never wasted. I have fond memories of the grocer's shop, although by today's standards it would probably be closed on the grounds of hygiene. Nothing was pre-wrapped, bacon was sliced and cheese and butter cut and weighed in front of the customer. Biscuits were taken from a large tin and put into paper bags on the scales, as were oats for our breakfast. The floor of the shop was well scrubbed floor-boards and the smells of the groceries would automatically make you feel hungry, nothing was pre-packed or triple wrapped. The prices also made shopping on a budget much easier, as the prices didn't vary from shop to shop or week to week!

Girlie, Fluffy and Blackie

Girlie the dog had an easy chair by the side of Mrs Ls bed. She was a poorly dog and seemed to suffer a lot from milk fever and canker in her ears. When the vet called she would cower behind a chair in the corner of the room and it would take a lot of time and patience to get her out, she was completely spoilt and extremely over-weight. She wore a medallion round her neck announcing that she was a member of 'The Tail Waggers Club' and each month a magazine would be delivered full of stories about other pampered pets, diets and doggy photographs. Out in the car, her favourite position was to have her hind legs on the back seat and her front paws on either side of Mr L's neck. On a summer's day she loved the wind blowing her ears away from her face, a truly spoilt dog.

There was a bi-annual event when Girlie came into season. We had a short drive to the front of the house and then a pathway along the side. The back garden had high fences all round. When the time came to protect Girlie from unwanted attention, Mr L had a large piece of three-ply board with a drawing of the map of the world on it, which he would secure to the side of the house at the end of the drive. Girlie had all the freedom of the side of the house and back garden, meaning everyone could relax in the knowledge that she was safe from the local (and some not so local) dogs being driven mad by her scent. There was one sad dog, a cross between a spaniel and a St Bernard, who would sit outside the gate for three weeks at a time. I don't know how he survived without nourishment for so long or why he didn't catch pneumonia. Sometimes he would be drenched to the skin for days on end, but nothing would budge him … what power there is in female hormones! One day he managed to jump the front gate, only to be met by the large tabby cat who seemed to think he was a guard dog when Girlie was indisposed. I've never seen a dog retreat at such a speed as he did on that day, but it didn't cool his ardour, he just kept watch at a safer distance! The down side of this was the stopping of doggy-walks; we were both kept away from male company for three weeks!

Another story about the pets concerned Blackie, the cat that was rescued from the garage. Fluffy was a hunter and earned his keep as a brilliant mouser, but his black sibling was lazy. One day Mr L was clearing the garage and found a nest of new-born mice. He told me to keep Fluffy indoors and bring out Blackie; he then placed the heaving mass of furless, sightless mice under Black-

ie's nose. He took one look and fled up the garden to hide from whence he'd started ... among the cabbages!

The wireless was used mainly for the news bulletins. It seemed as if peoples' lives revolved around the news, but we did have some light entertainment. Each lunch time we listened to 'Workers Playtime' which would be broadcast from various factories around the country, it was a mix of music and comedy. Sandy Wilson, with his plaintive *Can you hear me Mother?* and Arthur Askey singing his song *Buzz, buzz, buzz, buzz, honey bee, honey bee, buzz if you like but don't sting me.* Other names that spring to mind are Elsie and Doris Walters, their brother Jack Warner, Gracie Fields, whose version of the Maori *Song of Farewell* brought a tear to many an eye. Vera Lynn was extremely popular with her songs that touched the feelings of both the men away from home and their loved ones left behind. *There'll be Bluebirds over the White Cliffs of Dover* was as British as you could get. The Germans had their own song *Lily Marlene* and when Vera Lynn recorded it in English it became an immediate 'hit'. This upset the German Army who thought it was 'their' song. There were many more entertainers but their names escape me. At tea time we listened to children's hour with Uncle Mac relating the adventures of Larry the Lamb, his programme always ended with 'Goodnight children, everywhere'. I secretly believed he was speaking to me, telling me that I wasn't forgotten. A favourite evening programme was ITMA (*Its That Man Again*) with Tommy Handley and a multitude of other characters. How we laughed when Mrs Mopp said 'Can I do you now sir?' or Colonel Chinstrap's drunken 'I don't mind if I do'. There was a comedy half-hour with 'Old Mother Riley,' played by Arthur Lucan, and his Irish daughter Kitty, they were very funny. I would be in the kitchen doing my various chores, straining my ears to listen to the voices coming from the radio in the back sitting room. A boy at school had a comic called *Film Fun* and Arthur Askey and Old Mother Riley were some of the characters with their own comic strip. Another cause of humour on the radio was the propaganda broadcasts from Germany by 'Lord Haw-haw'. He was an American born Irishman working for the Nazis (real name James Joyce). We would first listen to the BBC News which we knew to be true and factual, then 'Lord Haw-haw' would come over the airways with his lies and propaganda messages. He started his broadcast with his adenoidal 'Germany calling, Germany calling', causing much amusement.

I was baby-sitting for a neighbour one evening and listening to a programme called *Appointment With Fear*. Valentine Dyall, called 'The Man in Black' had a very deep and chilling voice, he would create the scene and atmosphere for a radio play. I'll not forget *The Nutcracker Suite* ever! it scared the living daylights out of me! It was about a couple in a hotel suite who noticed the walls kept getting nearer and nearer to the bed and at the same time the ceiling was gradually getting lower and lower … creepy or not? Radio is far superior to television when you have to use your imagination. I had a vivid imagination! I got the feeling that Mr L would have preferred it if I'd been a boy, it was nothing unusual for him to wake me up as he passed my landing bed and ask me to accompany him downstairs to the kitchen. I'd sleepily follow him downstairs where, at four in the morning we would listen to a crackly commentary on boxing matches with Joe Louis, the American Heavyweight boxer, or pick up the music of the 'Grand Ol' Oprey'.

Chickens

We had chickens at the bottom of the garden, I believe the majority of households kept chickens as eggs and meat were rationed. I know we had one egg per person per week, which is not very much is it? They were more Joy's interest than mine, although I think we both had our share of boiling up the vegetable scraps and potato peelings, before mixing them with bran for their hot meal on winter mornings.

Ferrets

I had two ferrets and Mr L would take me, the dog and the ferrets into the country to shoot rabbits with his double-barrelled shotgun. We would stand in the middle of the field round about dusk to wait for the rabbits to show their heads above ground. Girlie was as good as a retriever, she would pick the rabbits up as they were shot and drop them at her master's feet. Ferreting was different, the ferret was released from the sack into a rabbit hole and Mr L would just wait and shoot the rabbits as they came out of their burrows further along the hedge. I thought it less sporting than relying on one's marksmanship. One day when I arrived home from school I found Mrs L sitting on an old tin trunk at the bottom of the garden, too scared to move. One of the ferrets had escaped from its hutch and although a neighbour had managed to pick it up and place it in the trunk, she was sure it would get out again if she moved. (It's true that all bullies are cowards.)

Rabbits

I acquired a pet white rabbit in a strange way. One morning Joy was late getting up, so I had to go across the road and throw stones at the window to wake her. I didn't want Mrs L to find out Joy hadn't started her chores. It was 6.30a.m. and the ground was covered in thick snow, the only other person around was the Postman and he was trying to catch a large, white buck rabbit. He finally caught it by its ears and handing it to me said 'Happy Christmas'. Joy had now joined me and we took the struggling bunny indoors to show Mr L. I told him it was a present from the Postman and I was allowed to keep it in the shed until a proper hutch could be made. It was strange living quarters for my pets, as I had a rabbit and two ferrets cohabiting in the same shed! … in separate hutches though, or the rabbit would have had a very short life, wouldn't he?

Sheep's head stew

One of the things we had to eat, which we don't see now, was sheep's head. It was made into a stew with turnips, parsnips, swedes and what I dreaded most, artichokes; no matter how I tried to acquire a taste for them they always seemed like cardboard-flavoured potatoes to me. The trouble was we were not allowed to leave any food on our plates (Girlie and I had an arrangement unknown to Mrs L, perhaps that's the reason she was so overweight). Now I come to think of it Granny L also loved the sheep's brains. We did have some very hot curries and I would try to eat each mouthful with rice to cool it down a bit, but I still drank a lot of cold water. Mrs L could however, make a delicious Yorkshire Pudding. I liked to scrape the bottom of the tin after everyone had been served; ummmm crispy and greasy.

The top of the milk

A delicacy that Joy and I would vie for was the top of the milk. I'll explain. We had to be registered with a certain dairy (and coal-man and butcher for that matter), the milk lady would have large churns of milk on her horse-drawn cart, the customer would hand her a jug and she'd use a pint measure to ladle the milk from the churn to the jug. As we had no fridge, the milk in the summer was scalded to stop it 'turning'; we did this by placing the jug in a large saucepan of water and bringing the water to the boil. When it had cooled down there was a thick skin of cream on the top of the jug … this is what we vied for; put it on a saucer, add a little sugar, mix it all together and … 'wow'!

Rations

Sugar, of course, was rationed and from the age of nine I stopped taking sugar in tea, When we visited someone's home and were offered a cup of tea it was thought impolite to say you took sugar. Once you've tasted tea without sweetening it tastes awful if you go back to it being sweetened. I don't recall the love of coffee that exists today, perhaps because it was Camp Coffee or nothing, which made tea the favourite beverage! The sugar ration was saved to make jam when fruit was available in the summer and autumn. Sometimes the milk did go sour and Granny L. showed me how to make cottage cheese. The sour milk was poured into a muslin bag, tied at the top and allowed to drip into the sink. When all the whey had drained through we would untie the bag, put the curds into a basin, add a little salt, beat with a fork and 'Hey Presto!' cottage cheese. With so small a cheese ration it certainly tasted good on bread. We didn't have butter, just margarine, Mrs L being the only person in the house to have the butter ration. We didn't go short of eggs however, as the chickens kept us well supplied. In fact we had large stone jars which we filled with eggs and poured over them a mixture called 'isinglass'. This preserved the eggs for us to use when the chickens weren't laying. I always thought it strange that when we had the new chicks they were fed on mashed up, hard boiled eggs and the older chickens seemed to enjoy pecking the bones of an old carcass. Cannibalism at its worst.

Eggs

Bread

The bread during the war was a dirty grey colour, but Mr L could get 'Hovis' for himself as he was a diabetic. I acquired my taste for bitter dark chocolate by eating some of Mr L's diabetic ration; sweets and chocolate were in short supply and Mr L's diabetic chocolate was the only available source. I also remember honey on the comb, it would run down onto the plate to be scooped up with my knife onto a thick door-step of bread. That killed the taste of the margarine! Mr L had a friend who was head dairy man on a large estate, and one evening he brought home some bottles of milk. Instead of half an inch of cream and the rest milk, these bottles were all cream apart from half an inch of milk at the bottom … delicious!

Keeping meat fresh was a problem without refrigerators. Outside in the garden was a meat safe – a wooden box with very fine mesh across the front, okay in the winter months but not very successful in summer. I can still smell meat that is not quite as fresh as it should be, but with rationing nothing was wasted. The meat would be soaked in vinegar, rinsed and then cooked. Mind you, if you smelt the meat before it was cooked it seemed to linger in your nostrils and you could taste it as you ate. **Meat**

The daily routine at the Ls was very harrowing. Everything that could be cleaned had to be cleaned. Outside in the back garden was an old table on which mats had to be brushed and vegetables prepared, lovely in warm weather but a nightmare to me when it was cold. I suffered from 'dead-fingers' and at the slightest drop in temperature my fingers would turn white, but instead of allowing the circulation to come back gradually, Mrs L would plunge my hands into a bowl of hot water. It was agony. **Daily routine**

Shortly after we were adopted, Mrs L was asked why she had taken on two girls, especially as they were at an awkward age for adoption. Joy and I have her reply imbedded in our brains like a micro-chip.

'Percy needed to save money on his Income Tax and I need help with the housework' was her reply – and she wanted us to call her 'Mother'! We learnt a way around this by saying 'Ma'am'.

Spring was not a welcoming in of warmer weather, or the leaves appearing on the trees and the flowers bursting into bloom, but the dreaded 'Spring-Cleaning'. Every rug, large and small had to be rolled up and taken into the garden, hung over the washing line and beaten thoroughly with the carpet-beater (a metal head on a long handle). This was not the time for Mrs L to lose her temper with such a handy weapon at her disposal, but then Mrs L was unpredictable. If we had worked out her reasons for suddenly flaring up we could have avoided them. All would be going along smoothly, when suddenly her eyes would start to bulge behind her steel-rimmed glasses, her teeth would clench … and a hiding would follow, not a time to say 'What' instead of 'Pardon'. She did say to Mr L that she had read somewhere that children should be caned at the back of the knees, but she forgot this if a more suitable tool came to hand, like the carpet-beater or Hoover tools. I even remember on one occasion when she started to beat me, Mr L stood between us and allowed her to rain blows on his back! At eleven years of age I thought he was extremely brave, but in retrospect, I realise he was a very weak man who could have done more to help us if he'd had more backbone. **Hidings**

One job I had which allowed me to day-dream was killing the ants on the front porch. Mrs L had a fear of ants getting into the kitchen, so if I wanted to **Ants** get outside for a while I would tell her I'd seen an ant in the hall. Armed with a bottle of ammonia and cotton wool, I could spend half an hour idly sitting on the front porch looking for any ants that might scurry across. Pooh … ammonia does pong!

The bathroom had to be scrupulously clean. Mr L had a glass trolley on which he kept his phials of insulin and glass dishes of peroxide containing his hypodermic needles. I decided I would like my mousy-coloured hair to be blonde like the American Film stars. Each day while cleaning the bathroom, I would dip a piece of cotton wool in peroxide and rub it across my fringe. I was asked once if I'd dyed my hair but I insisted it was made lighter by the sun. A couple of other things that were always in the bathroom were 'Bay-Rum' which Mr L used on his hair and 'Bile-Beans' which were taken as laxatives. They worked eventually, but not until you'd suffered a belly-ache for several hours. When I was with my family Mother gave us 'Ex-Lax' which was much more pleasant, just like eating a piece of chocolate.

There were so many ways to get into Mrs L's bad books it seemed an impossible task at times not to stay out of trouble. The beds were scrupulously examined to make sure the 'hospital corners' were done properly, the pillows had to have their openings turned away from the door and fingers were poked into every nook and cranny for the slightest spec of dust. Even today, old as I am, I get tense if the house is untidy or finger marks are found on the doors or light-switches. Staying out of trouble was as easy as walking through a mine-field.

The allotment

I began to realise that gardening was a way to get out of the house, so I'd accompany Mr L when he went to work on the allotment; it was very therapeutic. There was one old man on one of the plots who would give me a stick of his 'Cherry Rhubarb,' it was deliciously sweet and a good thirst-quencher. I also managed to get away from the house to tend the graves of Pop and Charlie. I would take the dog with me and a pair of sheep-shearing scissors to trim the grass. I also used these scissors to trim the front lawn, it was a painstaking task but again I was outside the house. We didn't have a lawn-mower.

I had a lesson in how not to let your figure go. Mrs L had an elderly relative to stay for a week and after a few days I was asked to run her a bath. Oh how I hated that gas geyser! I had visions of being blown sky-high with that thing. Bath ready, the lady asked if I would stay and wash her back, I wasn't prepared for what happened next. Her breasts were two long empty sacks of skin, hanging down to her waist with a lump at the bottom. She then proceeded to throw them over her shoulder while she soaped and rinsed the front of her body, brought them back from whence they came, to dangle while I washed her back. Since that day, as soon as I started to develop 'bumps', my Bra. has been a vital garment when dressing!

**Dismal
Christmases**

I'm afraid to say that Christmases in Salisbury have prevented me from getting into the Christmas spirit ever! School didn't break-up until Christmas Eve, then we would go shopping in Woolworth's to buy presents. Mr L always managed to acquire an ox tongue, this was cooked and served cold on Christmas Eve after Midnight Communion. We had to go to Holy Communion again on Christmas morning, even though I couldn't partake in the services as I hadn't yet been confirmed. When we arrived home we were given our presents, ninety-nine percent clothes and a beautifully embroidered handkerchief sachet or some such from Mrs M next door. We were not allowed to show or discuss our presents with anyone, which seemed very odd to say the least, until we found out the reason. They were all stolen from parcels at the sorting-office. The remainder of Christmas Day was spent in the kitchen preparing vegetables, cooking, waiting at table, washing up, then like any ordinary Sunday the dreaded oven-cleaning, and mainly trying to keep out of trouble. The only difference was the Raisin Wine from the old lady two doors away; after a couple of glasses things looked much brighter.

Mr L worked for the Post Office and during November and December he was the night supervisor at the sorting office. Each morning as soon as he came home, he would empty his pockets of clothes, tins of fruit and anything else that had caught his fancy. His explanation was that 'all the parcels were damaged in transit and therefore he brought the contents home rather than see them wasted'. It all came to a head one morning when the Police arrived and searched the pantry. They found tins of 'Del Monte' fruit. He lost his job!

The old lady who lived two doors away was the widow of a school master, and it appeared Mr L had offered to help sort out her finances when her husband died. Being a child I don't honestly know what was involved, but I did hear the phrase 'heard in camera', which pleased Mrs L as the case wouldn't be reported in the newspapers. The outcome of this was a visit by the bailiffs; they **The bailiffs** stripped the house of everything, except that blasted, hated, wardrobe bed; it would appear Mrs L had the receipt in her name and not her husband's. In spite of their protests of injustice Mrs L went shopping in Southampton the next day and within a week the house was fully furnished again and all the receipts were in her name!

I do miss the sight of the Telegraph Boys. They looked so smart in their pill- **The Telegraph** box hats and red and navy blue uniforms, riding through the town on their red **Boys** bicycles. There was always a feeling of excitement when they delivered a telegram and waited to see if there was a reply. There was of course a downside to this if you had a husband, son or loved one serving in the Forces. The Telegraph Boy was then a harbinger of bad news, either 'Missing' or 'Killed in Action'. I recall the young wife of a paratrooper standing at her garden gate to receive a telegram and watched as she literally crumpled and fled indoors in tears. Her husband took part in the big parachute drop at Arnhem, never to return. It made the situation Joy and I found ourselves in very insignificant by comparison to all the misery that was taking place in the world.

It seemed strange to notice the lack of iron fencing and gates, which were an integral part of grand houses and they now looked open and bare, as the

Iron recycling

much needed iron was commandeered by the government to be melted down for ammunition. Early re-cycling really.

The Doctor

A visit to the doctor pre-NHS (National Health Service) was very different to today. We had to pay the sum of five shillings per visit, maybe that's the reason one doctor could run the practice single-handed. I can only recall two trips to the surgery. The first was because I suffered from very bad chesty coughs and Mr L's remedies were not working. When I had a particularly bad fit of coughing in the night, he gave me either a sugar lump soaked in eucalyptus or a teaspoonful of brandy. I thought they both tasted equally awful. The L's tired of me disturbing the whole household's sleep and took me to the doctor. Both Joy and I had 'cold injections', but as there was no known cure for the common cold, I don't know what we were injected with. We both agree however, that the reason we've escaped 'flu' epidemics and heavy colds throughout our adult life might be due to these jabs, who knows?

The second visit was as a teenager. I suffered incapacity every month with my periods. I spent many a morning at school lying down in the sick-room clutching a hot-water bottle. When I started work it was not unusual for my boss to order a taxi to take me home. A visit to the doctor seemed necessary. The tablets he prescribed were extremely large, made of rice-paper with a bitter yellow powder inside. Again I have no idea what they were, but they worked. I'd started menstruation when I was a couple of months away from my twelfth birthday, which was a bit of a shock as I didn't know why I was suddenly bleeding. Mrs L told me to see Joy who promptly told me I'd have to put up with this for the rest of my life! No other explanation. She showed me where to look for the pieces of linen in the airing cupboard, how to fold them to get the tapes in the correct position and a piece of ribbon to thread through the tapes. When I needed to change the 'towel' I had to soak the used one in cold water before putting it in the copper boiler for washday. Mrs.L refused to waste money on bought towels! When I received my first pay-packet I went to Boots to buy some 'proper towels', but I was so embarrassed that I waited ages until the male assistant was busy and I could be served by a female.

Mr L became very ill with glandular fever and a note was sent to the doctor asking him to make a house-visit (still no telephone). This would be more expensive, but because of his diabetes he had to be extra careful with his health. He was admitted to Salisbury Infirmary for three weeks. The day the doctor called I was feeling pretty sick myself, my throat was sore and my glands badly swollen, but even though the doctor was actually in the house, he was not asked to see me. Then one day Mr L arrived home from a stint on the allotment on the back of a horse and cart; one of the other men put him on it to bring him home when he found Mr L unconscious on the ground. He had forgotten to take a sugar lump with him and was in a diabetic coma, again he was admitted to Salisbury Infirmary for three weeks while they stabilised his insulin and sugar levels.

Mrs L suffered every winter with chilblains on the back of her legs and her great fear was that the skin would break and cause an infection; so one winter's day another note was sent to the surgery to ask the doctor to call. (You don't miss the telephone if you've never had one.) He suggested two remedies:- one, soak her feet in urine, or two, have two bowls of water, one hot the other cold and plunge the feet alternately into each. I was summoned to fill the two bowls of water and although she complained noisily she was assured it was doing her good. I don't think the doctor liked her very much, I recall him muttering as he left 'Must be a full moon again'.

Joy was ill, she kept getting repeat bouts of tonsilitis and the doctor sent her to hospital to have her tonsils removed. She was seventeen years old and it took her a long time to recover. She was so pale and thin that again I thought for a while that she had the dreaded TB. She didn't thank goodness, she was just desperately unhappy.

The big health worry in the 1940s was not malnutrition, as you would **TB** expect with food shortages, but Tuberculosis (TB). My school friend's father was in the TB hospital on Harnham Hill. He didn't recover and died before the war ended. During my time at Grammar School five girls died of this disease; it seemed to me the prettier the girl the more likely she was to became a victim of this terrible illness. Granny L's daughter was courting a man who lived further up the road, they'd met when she'd visited her Mother. He'd had TB and when we visited their house I had this crazy idea that if I sniffed his coat hanging in the hall, I would become infected. I don't think I seriously wanted to die, just be ill for a while and go into hospital for a rest and some 'T.L.C.' (tender loving care).

My main dread was the dentist. I still had the idea that all dentists were the same as the Army tooth-pullers, but when your tooth is aching there's no alternative but to get it treated. I'm sure I had more fillings and extractions than the average youngster. The drills made an awful noise and there were no injections to deaden the pain … and what a pain when he accidentally touched a nerve. When a tooth had to be extracted it felt as if the top of my head was being pulled off as well.

Today I have a dentist who never causes me pain and yet as soon as I sit in the chair rigor mortis sets in!

The church still played a big part in my life, despite the fact that I would fer- **Church** vently pray to God, Jesus and the Holy Spirit (in case I got it the wrong way round) to let me return home, deliverance was not forthcoming. I would lock myself in the bathroom to pray earnestly for my Mother to come and get me. I was told the sins of the fathers were visited upon the children, but I thought my punishment was a bit severe and it was time for me to be re-united with my family. I couldn't understand what terrible sin my Father had committed for me to have such a long punishment.

We went to Church every Sunday night, which was very different to the services I'd attended with my parents. St Michael's in Roman Road was very 'High Church', it was really only a church hall as the parish was waiting for a new church to be built, and the seats were just ordinary chairs put there for the service. The parishioners would cross themselves and bend their knees before going to their seats and it seemed to me to be very ritualistic. I had to learn the 'Nunc Dimitus' and the 'Magnificat'; even the hymns were different to the ones I'd learnt as a young girl. I was under the impression it was just a good excuse to show-off the ladies' new outfits, or who was wearing the smartest hat. I also hated the fact that Mrs L always insisted on sitting in the front row. I enjoyed walking to church with Granny L when she was alive as her long black skirt would rustle with every step she took – a wonderfully feminine sound. Things started to improve when we had a new and younger vicar called the Revd White. He upset a lot of the older members of the congregation by setting up a youth club and Sunday School. It was also quite amusing one Sunday when he said at the beginning of his sermon that he made no apologies for going to the Cinema to see Margaret Lockwood and James Mason (oooooh James Mason's voice was like molasses dripping off a spoon) in *The Wicked Lady*. It appears somebody had seen him and written a letter of complaint to the Bishop of Salisbury.

The Revd White was a very good influence in my life. Mrs L had this idea that vicars, doctors etc. were important people and should be treated with deference – an example of her respectable façade. She even had a phase where she was 'saved', she went to one of those tent crusades where they ask you to sign up for membership to God. It didn't change anything at home but I had to stand with her in the Market Square and try to recruit new members. At twelve years of age I was truly embarrassed. Her new religious fervour lasted three weeks. When I was thirteen, I became a Sunday School teacher to a class of young boys aged six to seven and thoroughly enjoyed the experience. I seemed popular with my pupils and they would draw a picture each week to illustrate the previous week's lesson. There was a lot of rivalry to please me and be rewarded with a star for the best picture. This required a good memory on my part as every child would at some time earn the coveted star. There was also a youth club, we acted in plays in the Church-Hall, had socials and I could even go to the Vicarage for Bible Classes to learn the Catechism in preparation for my Confirmation. The socials were more like a get-together, not like the discos of today, we'd play silly games like 'spin-the-bottle', 'pass-the-parcel', 'postman's-knock', 'forfeits' or talk for a minute in the centre of a circle without hesitating. Sometimes we would read plays, each taking a character. The cost of these activities was nil, but the enjoyment priceless.

One week there was to be a fancy-dress party in the Church-Hall for the members of the youth club, a prize would be awarded for the best costume. Joy had a long dress with ribbons draped around the hem to give a hooped effect, she called herself 'Little Bo-Peep'. I was really excited, I had a 'Harlequin' costume, yellow and black diamonds on a white background, a sort of 'Andy-

Pandy' style. I kept looking at it folded carefully in the airing-cupboard and getting more and more excited as the day of the party drew nearer. When the evening finally arrived I ran upstairs to have a bath and get changed when ... Mrs L said I had to stay at home. I stared in disbelief, which resulted in a clout across the head for impudence. Joy was allowed to go and won first prize for her costume! Another of Mrs L's ways of playing us one off against the other. Mr L gave me ten shillings! I always had money to spend as Mr L often gave me money after a particularly bad thrashing. I used to spend it on doughnuts for myself and friends on the way to school. I think I was trying to buy popularity.

The Revd White was taking a group of fourteen to fifteen year olds to a summer school in Devon. It was organised by youth clubs from all over the West of England. Joy was fifteen years old but I was only thirteen, however (and I don't know how he managed it) I was allowed to go. A whole week away! Unbelievable! We travelled by train to Devon and my first surprise was the redness of the soil as we passed through Somerset, it was such a contrast to the chalky white soil of Salisbury. When we arrived at Shute House (our home for the next seven days) we were allocated dormitories, boys upstairs and the girls one floor below. The sense of freedom was incredible. Although every minute of each day was organised, to Joy and me it was teenage heaven! There was a lot of banter between the sexes, but in those days it was always harmless fun. When we arrived I found a vase of flowers had been left in the dormitory, the stagnant water smelt absolutely foul. I stuck my head out of the window and called the name of one of the boys, as soon as his head appeared above me I tossed the putrid liquid up to his face, he was not amused. He was to get his revenge! One day we were having a fight on the bed in the dormitory and the springs gave way, we fell through the hole and landed on the floor, much to the amusement of everyone else. Luckily there was a spare bed at the end of the room, so we swopped it for mine and none of the adults were any the wiser. The girls also learnt early in the week to inspect their beds before getting into them as they were often booby-trapped with dead mice or teazles, or re-made in 'apple-pie' fashion. The first morning was Sunday and after Matins in the small chapel we went on a seven mile walk. All was well until we came to a field with a bull in it. Joy wouldn't cross it as she was wearing a red dress, so I went ahead and she followed. ... It was a very uninterested bull!

We took a train to Beer from Seaton station (which cost sixpence) and spent a day on the beach. While we were there one of the girls suggested we have a midnight feast. We pooled our B.U's (short for bread-units, as bread and cakes were now rationed), bought more sticky buns than bread and hoped we wouldn't get caught. We turned all the beds round to make a circle and on the dot of midnight started our feast. We'd bought some candles and placed them on saucers in the centre of the ring so that we could see what we were doing without being seen. Such a simple thing to do, but knowing it was against the rules made it doubly exciting.

I went mackerel fishing in a small boat with my sister, the vicar and half a dozen choir boys. It seemed a good idea at the time. I was fine watching the water while trailing my hand in the sea, but wishing I hadn't eaten so much dinner. I turned my head to look at one of the lads and his face had turned green! I had never seen a green face before. Suddenly I was as sick as I never believed possible. Joy informs me I was very green! On the last evening a concert was arranged in the school's own small theatre. The Revd White announced that he had a request for me, it was 'I do like to be beside the seaside'. Very droll! One of the girls and one of the boys sang a duet of Ivor Novello songs and very good they sounded. I often wondered what became of them, probably joined an amateur operatic society or something.

I discovered a strange thing about mice. One morning as I was walking along the hall to the dining-room, I saw a cat with a mouse in its mouth. The poor thing was squeaking so pitifully that I grabbed its tail hoping the cat would release it. I was left with a tail! In future I'd let nature take its course, as by interfering I had prolonged the mouse's agony. Even the weather was kind to us that week, it rained while we were asleep and the sun shone during the day. After a brilliant seven days that seemed to fly by, it was time to return home.

In spite of everything that was happening in my life, I did manage to pass the 'Eleven Plus' exam and after an interview with Miss Moore, the head mistress of South Wilts Grammar School, I was accepted as a pupil. I think I was extremely lucky with my interview, the other girls said they were asked to do mental arithmetic and went through what they described as 'the third degree'. My experience was completely different, I had to spell 'dahlia', 'chrysanthemum' and 'precipice', I'm not even sure I spelt them correctly. The head-mistress then asked if I played chess, when I replied 'I only play draughts' she spent the rest of the allotted time explaining the game of chess to me. Lucky? Yes I think I was. The success of passing the 'Eleven Plus' was down to the excellent ground work done by the Army schools and later at Highbury Avenue School by Mr Ayres.

My first terms at Grammar School had to be paid for, each parent paid a fee according to their income, but after the 1944 Butler Act, Grammar School education was free to every child. My biggest problem now was how to fit in homework with the chores … not an easy thing to do. Although I never aspired to the 'A' stream, I avoided the 'C' stream and coped reasonably well in the 'B' stream. All the teachers were elderly spinsters and the school was single sex. There was a shortage of young teachers as most of them were either working in the munitions factories, serving in the Land Army, or in the Armed Services.

SWGS 25th Anniversary

The strangest sight I've ever seen was on the 25th anniversary of the school. The Guildhall was booked for a dinner and dance for five hundred girls plus female teachers. We danced to a hired band and were all beautifully dressed in full length evening gowns. The boys were outside on the Guildhall steps waiting to escort us home. The dress I most remember belonged to a Prefect, she wore a white gown with hand-painted red roses around the hem, it was really beautiful. I was lucky enough to wear the dress I'd worn as a bridesmaid several months before.

The ruse to keep us away from male influences wasn't very successful. The boys' Grammar School was to the south of the market square and the girls' school to the north so the inevitable clandestine meetings took place in the centre of town. As we boarded the bus to go home, the boys would carry our heavy satchels on their bikes. They'd cycle behind the bus and compete over whose wheel could be placed nearest to the bus platform … very dangerous. The buses, because of the petrol shortage, towed a strange gas contraption behind them and instead of the usual trade advertisements we'd read, 'Coughs and Sneezes spread Diseases' and 'Careless Talk Costs Lives'. The advertisement that sticks in my mind the most was on a large billboard. A lady was carrying a baby, she wore a black cape with a hood covering her face and written in big letters underneath was 'VD Kills'. I always thought it was some sort of bomb used by Hitler. On a lighter note, the hoarding which made me smile showed a picture of a short, fat man with a tin of 'Andrews Liver Salts' sticking out of his back pocket – the caption read 'I think I've left something behind'.

The Boys' Grammar School

School buses

The Grammar School itself was a catchment area for a number of villages surrounding Salisbury. The City was situated in a valley and was prone to unbelievably dense fogs. You really could not see your hand in front of your face, I know this for a fact as I've tried it. The children from the outlying districts had their buses cancelled when the fogs came down and the town children would be sent home. We also had a strange period when Portsmouth Grammar School was evacuated *en-masse* to Salisbury. To cope with the overload we alternated mornings and afternoons, catching up on our lessons with extra homework. I found it easier to make friends at Grammar School. My best friend, Renee, lived in the nearby village of Barford-St-Martin and I was not asked to visit after school or at weekends, unlike Junior school where it made me seem unfriendly, the truth being that I was not allowed out after school. I would have liked to have played Lacrosse for the school team but knew I wouldn't be able to take part in weekend matches or after-school practice, so I under-achieved … it seemed the easier option.

The teachers were excellent and stretched our minds to the limit. The Geography mistress showed us slides she had taken on her travels in the 1920s giving us an insight into distant places and peoples, making us feel that travel was a 'must-do-that' when we grew up. Unfortunately, after the war all the magic was taken away by Western influences, sky-scrapers everywhere!

Geography

Mademoiselle was a delightful character, I think she came to England to escape the German Invasion. She would appear in the classroom wearing layers and layers of clothes and never removed her coat whatever the climate; she had a small mouth but always wore very bright red lipstick with a pronounced

French

'cupid's bow', and wore her gingery coloured hair twisted into a tight knot at the nape of her neck. Before the lesson we would open all the windows (aren't kids cruel when they spot a weakness?) – her first words on entering the class were always 'Fermez les fenêtres, mes enfants'. We were each given a French name equivalent to our own, but there were quite a few 'Jeans' in the class so I was called 'Lucille', I rather liked that name. We also acted out French songs and I often had the task of doing the dialogue, evidently I had a good French accent.

Music

Miss Walpole, the Music teacher, was auditioning for the school choir and Renee and I thought we'd give it a try; she had a good voice and sang regularly in her village church choir, whereas I could never class myself as a singer, it sounded excellent in my head but not to everyone else's ears. We had been told that how you levelled your voice in the years twelve to sixteen would develop the pitch throughout adulthood and we admired the husky tones of Marlene Dietrich; we talked in as deep a tone as we could thinking it sounded the epitome of femininity. We managed a place in the choir to sing in Handel's Messiah in St. Francis church, but not among the sopranos, oh no! we sang the low melody 'O Sacred Head sore wounded' ... it was most enjoyable though.

Gym

The Gym was another area of delight. Climbing wall frames or ropes, vaulting the horse or doing mat exercises were all good ways of releasing tension. I also enjoyed showing off by doing hand-stands, cart-wheels and my 'piece-de-resistance' the crab; whereas most girls did the crab by pushing up from the ground, I found I could achieve it from the standing position and bending over backwards ... cocky little madam that I was! I was asked by the PT (physical training) teacher if she could photograph me during the lunch break, she seemed to think I was good at vaulting the 'horse'. I have one regret, I never saw the pictures. One day Renee and I changed into our PT kit early (fetching little numbers that resembled a skater's dress, in green and white check and matching knickers), as the gym was empty we decided to climb the ropes and do Tarzan impressions. Unfortunately for us, we were in full throttle when the headmistress, Miss Moore, walked in! We were ordered to change back into uniform and wait in her ante-room. This was bad news. We were both threatened with expulsion and had to write two-hundred lines saying 'I will not swing on the ropes'!

Sex education

We did receive 'sex-education' ... well I think we did. The second year all gathered in the assembly hall, the lights were put out and on the platform stood an elderly gentleman. He showed us lantern-slides of boys without clothes on, using a pointer to explain the difference between the genitals of males and females, not much else really. When the lights went on again he asked if we had any questions to ask him. No-one answered. Then he asked if any girls had started their periods. No-one answered. We'd learnt more about sex in Biology classes studying the reproductive organs of a rabbit! The Head-Mistress had a habit of doing a spot check after school to see if the inside of our desks was tidy. She just happened to do one the day of the sex lecture; one of the girls had a 'dirty poem' in her desk and Miss Moore discovered it. The next day the poor girl had to sit through the lecture again, on her own, as she obviously hadn't understood. It was doubly embarrassing knowing the Boys' Grammar School was having their lecture on the same day. I don't know how theirs differed from ours, but the new catch-word among the boys was 'It only takes nine minutes'. In their dreams!

One thing I always coveted at school was a 'The Red Sash'. These were worn with pride by prefects and awarded to pupils for sports excellence, deportment, tidy desks, elocution, gardening the form's plot, good attendance and anything else that shouted you're better than the others at something. (The Head Girl even had 'bars' on hers, which meant she was 'excellent' several times over). No matter how erect I walked, or how hard I tried to speak without a Wiltshire accent, my name was never called during prize-giving at the end of each year. I was also pretty good at gardening and spent most lunch breaks planting seeds and weeding the form's plot ... but no Red Sash! My desk was a model of tidiness and good order ... no Red Sash!. My only moment of glory came from an unexpected source; I collected money for Dr. Barnado's Homes, thinking it would help my brothers. I organised plant and clothing sales during morning breaks and I was awarded a Silver Shield by Barnados ... but not a Red Sash!

The Red Sash

One of the girls had been away from school for some while. She'd had an operation for appendicitis and we all signed a card to wish her well. We were taken aback however when her Father sent an invitation to the whole class to come for tea on the following Saturday, and even supplied the transport. As the invitation was for everyone I was allowed to go, but I was unprepared for the difference in this girl's life to mine. She had her own Grand Piano on a raised dais in the music room. In the garden the tea was laid out for forty girls and even more mouth-opening, (or gob-smacking in today's parlance) an ice-cream van hired for the day! It was most impressive.

Before I go on to anything new, I would like to mention some of the traditions of South Wilts. The badge on our green blazers depicted the five rivers in the valley of Salisbury, by five silver lines on a green background. Underneath was the word 'Onwards'. The names of the rivers were Nadder, Wylie, Avon, Ebble and Bourne. The first verse of the school song, written by Miss Hart the History teacher, went as follows:

SWGS traditions

> 'Widely yet the five streams flow,
> Fails the green plain never,
> As from age to age we go,
> Onward, onward ever'.

At the end of every morning assembly we sang,

> 'God be in my head, and in my understanding,
> God be in my eyes, and in my looking,
> God be in my mouth, and in my speaking,
> God be at my end, and at my departing'.

They're thoughtful words to start the day.

Uniform

During the first two years our uniform comprised green gymslips, white blouses, green tie with silver stripes, awful terracotta woollen stockings, green blazer, green mackintosh, brown shoes, and finally, to top the lot, a black velour hat with a hat-band similar to the tie. The shoes were called 'bar-shoes' because they had a strap across the centre which was fastened by a button, to make this easier we used a button hook. In summer the gymslips were changed to green and white gingham check dresses, white knee length socks and brown sandals, the velour hat being replaced by a straw Panama hat. I wished we could have the straw boaters worn by the girls of the Godolphin School, very chic I thought. I think I should mention here that undergarments in winter consisted of vest, liberty bodice, petticoat, and bloomers with a handkerchief pocket at the bottom of the leg. In the summer we wore green check cotton knickers and a petticoat. When we became seniors we were allowed to wear lisle stockings instead of the woollen ones and skirts replaced the awful gymslips. I remember turning up for school one day in a red check dress, my school dress was still in the wash, and I was promptly sent home to change. The rules regarding uniform were very rigid. The dresses we wore were slightly shorter than knee length, then Christian Dior announced his 'New Look' or 'A-Line' in 1948. We had debates at school, being divided into pro and con long clothes in this modern day. I was totally against the 'New Look'. I was very tall and instead of the skirts reaching my ankle bone as Dior designed they should, they ended mid-calf, while my friends of average height wore the new length as Dior had intended it to be worn.

Prefects

Prefects had a great deal of power both in school and out. They would monitor our behaviour on the bus journey home and in the town, if we were found to be doing anything that brought shame to our uniform, names were taken and then read out during next morning's assembly. We were not allowed to eat in the street and that included sucking a sweet!, nor were we to be seen talking to a member of the opposite sex. We were proud to be wearing the green uniform and were expected to behave accordingly.

I would like to mention here (going off at a tangent again!) that swearing was not part of our vocabulary; the worst word we heard was 'damn' and the nearest I came to uttering it was 'darn'. I've tried to remember if the soldiers or local lads swore, but I can't recall any of them swearing, unlike the language of the 1990s which grates on the ears of my generation … Pity! I remember an incident at Larkhill when I was still with my Mother, I'd keep saying, 'Gor Blimey'.

All the correcting and telling off seemed to make me use the phrase more and more, it just slipped out. My Mother was at the end of her patience and said,

'Do you know what you are saying? You are asking God to blind you.'

I stopped saying 'Gor Blimey'.

School photo

There was some nervousness on the day of the school photograph. I had a blouse made from parachute silk, it felt lovely and soft to the skin, however someone had heard that if you're wearing parachute silk for a photograph you come out naked! (don't ask me how these rumours start) so until the day of truth I was pretty concerned. I needn't have worried, I looked the same as everyone else. I was baffled however by the fact that we stood in a half-circle and the end result was a straight line!

They say that school days are the best days of your life and as far as I was concerned, they were. I thoroughly enjoyed my time at South Wilts and was very sad when I had to leave.

One Friday afternoon in September 1946 I decided I didn't want to go home after school, to go through the routine of bedroom cleaning, punishments and nagging which had now become a way of life, only to get into more strife back at school on Monday for not completing my homework. It was a lovely late summer evening, I had sixpence in one blazer pocket and a rock cake in the other. I headed towards London. I had no plans for when I finally arrived in the City, it just seemed the right place to go as I believed Dr Barnado's was there and I could meet up with my brothers. I hadn't walked far when a car stopped and the driver asked if I'd like a lift as far as Stockbridge. I climbed into the back seat thinking how much further I could travel by car instead of my expected slow progress by 'Shankses Pony'. The driver and his wife were a

Going AWOL

middle-aged couple who asked where I was heading. I told them, 'London' … they didn't ask 'why?', as if it was a normal occurrence for thirteen year olds, wearing school uniform, to walk from Salisbury to the Capital. They dropped me off on the outskirts of Stockbridge and waved as they drove away. I started walking … and walked and walked.

It was dusk when I reached a village called Micheldever. I was feeling pretty hungry, my rock cake but a distant memory. As I walked down the road, I noticed two men leaning over a farm gate and deep in conversation. As I drew level one of the men looked up and asked me where I was going. I told him 'London'. 'It's a bit late' he said, 'Would you like something to eat and somewhere to sleep? You can sleep in my daughter's bed for the night and then continue your journey tomorrow'.

I was just about dead on my feet, I'd been up since half past six that morning and it was now past nine o'clock at night, so food and sleep seemed too good an offer to refuse. I had the best Ploughman's Supper ever, thick bread and margarine, with a huge wedge of cheese and pickles, washed down with a cold glass of milk. I dragged myself up the stairs and slid into bed by the side of a sound asleep girl (she must have been surprised when she woke up!). I was in the land of nod before the count of 'two'.

I came downstairs in the morning to a room full of policemen. The farmer apologised to me, but explained that he'd feared for my safety as a further one hundred yards up the road was a POW (Prisoner of War) camp. The police took me by car to Winchester police station. I sat in a cell (doors open) eating sausage and mash on a tin plate, and drank tea from a tin mug. It really tasted good and the policemen were being very friendly. Eventually, Mr Braggar the NSPCC man arrived and I was driven back to the L's. No-one asked me why I had run away? For the next two days no smacks. I was even allowed to go to the cinema to see *Pinocchio*, I wished I could whistle to bring help when in trouble, Jimminy Cricket and I would have been best mates. Back at school on Monday I was summoned to Miss Moore's inner sanctum, she asked me why I hadn't talked to her about my problems. (When you're daily told of worse fates to befall you, you don't complain!) However, my homework was reviewed more favourably and we had periods at school when we could do some catching up. Running away hadn't been quite fruitless, but it didn't solve the real problem.

Olympics 1948

There was great excitement in the summer of 1948. The Olympic Games were to be held in London and the Olympic Torch would be carried through Salisbury. We lined the road at Skew Bridge, on the Wilton Road, and cheered when the runner appeared proudly bearing the Olympic Torch above his head. I'm ashamed to admit I don't recall the name of the runner.

Boys

I discovered I liked boys! Stranger still was the fact that boys seemed to like me! There was Mrs L telling me day in and day out that I was ugly and gauche, my hair was akin to rats'-tails, my hips were too large, my Mother didn't want me and anything else she could think of to lower my feeling of well-being. Never-the-less, boys liked me, I found that here was the human affection I craved. Boys liked to hold hands, put an arm round my shoulders or waist, it was not complicated and they reminded me of my brothers! Boy/girl relationships were so innocent and uncomplicated in the 1940s, I'd never heard of 'tonsil-tickling' or 'tongues', although someone told me about 'French' kissing and that sounded pretty disgusting. Our progress with boys was more a journey of discovery, finding out about emotions step by step. I feel sorry for the young people today when relationships are so intense, I liken it to reading the last page of a book before knowing the plot! When I reached my early 'teens' I re-arranged the route for walking the dog. Instead of the designated route to the allotments I would go up the road as expected, then down the next, heading for Bemerton recreation ground where all the youngsters would congregate by the river. As dogs don't tell tales, dog-walking was much more fun! A boy I had been friendly with for nearly three years was going out with a senior girl from my school and he told me she allowed him to put his hand inside her bra, I was shocked and each day when I saw her at school I would think 'You're a trollop, I know about you and what you do with boys'! One lad had a pet monkey, it always seemed to be escaping up the church tower. One day I offered the monkey an onion, I'd been reliably informed he would eat anything, don't you believe it ... he peeled back the skin, took a sniff and promptly threw it at my head!

Ice-cream

A story went round the school like wildfire, ice-cream was on sale in a restaurant in town. We did a detour on the way home and each of us ordered 'sixpenny worth'. We sat expectantly at the table until the waitress bought it to us on a saucer, it was like the stuff on the freezer when it needs de-frosting! but we had been five years without the taste of ice-cream and thought it was supposed to taste like water with lumps of ice in it ... very similar to Sorbet, but without any flavour!

Books

I had access to a number of books both at the L's and Aunt May's, and I became an avid reader of anything I could lay my hands on, it was a wonderful form of escapism. I remember being moved to tears by *Uncle Tom's Cabin* and felt very romantic reading a love story called, *The Garden of Allah*. I was so impressed by the hero in the latter that I swore I would call my son Boris (I think Simon must be relieved that I changed my mind). However, the book that stayed in my memory to this day had pictures only. It was called *Lest We Forget*. It contained photographs taken by the Allied Forces as they marched into the internment camps at Belsen and Auschwitz. The horrendous images were imprinted on my mind forever, justifying the feelings of hate for Hitler and knowing it was right to fight a War that finally brought about the defeat of the Nazis.

Food and clothes were still in short supply and difficult to obtain. At the age of fourteen I had an added problem, feet that were growing too large! Mr L took me to Moores, the Clark's retail shop in Salisbury, to buy new shoes. When my feet were measured and the shop assistant discovered I needed size eight, she sent me to the men's department. I can't explain how humiliating this felt to a girl my age. For the next few years I pushed my feet into size sevens. I still have the crippling bunions to prove it!

My first Ball

Mr L belonged to the 'Loyal Order of Moose' and he had risen to some dizzy height in this organisation. There was to be the Annual Dinner and Ball at the Guildhall, several of the local dignitaries had been invited and I was chosen to present a bouquet to the Mayoress. I was dressed in my best clothes and can remember wearing silver sandals (no recollection of my dress though). I curtsied and handed over the bouquet, but the next bit was more difficult. When I sat down to dinner, the only child in the room, I stared at the array of cutlery at each place setting, there appeared to be more than seemed necessary for one person. I felt quite panic stricken. On my left sat a young man in his early twenties, he bent forward and whispered: 'Start at the outside and work your way in'.

As each course arrived, he would smile and pick up his cutlery first as if to make sure I didn't make a mistake. He had my eternal gratitude, he talked to me continually throughout the meal and even danced with me later in the evening. I don't remember his name, but his kindness was much appreciated by this gauche teenager.

Fordingbridge

One day, Mr L took me to Fordingbridge, a small village on the edge of the New Forest, to visit a shop that sold wooden animals carved by ex-soldiers. He bought a Huntsman, resplendent in his red jacket, and another in a green jacket and two Beagle Hounds. They were beautifully made and I often wondered what became of them; his final purchase was 'The House That Jack Built' The details of each figure were a work of art in themselves, all the characters were made to scale, from Jack himself to the tiny mouse that ate the corn. It was truly wonderful craftsmanship.

Silly songs

I thought I would record some of the silly songs I learnt as a child that seemed to have been forgotten since 'Pop Music' came into vogue, not nursery rhymes, as they are well documented. The silliest one first taught to me by Mr L went:

    'Alleluia skin a donkey, cut his tail off, amen'. Next,
    'A wonderful bird is a Pelican,
    His beak holds more than his belly can,
    He sits on the grass, With his beak up his ——,
    I wonder how the hell he can',
Lastly,
    'Chin chin Chinaman bought a penny doll,
    Washed it, dressed it, the doctor couldn't come,
    Because he had a pain in his tum tum tum'.

The first popular song I learnt from the radio was the 'Umbrella Song' sung by 'Flanagan and Allen, I think I liked all the 'Doodle-oom- a-loom-a, -doodle-oom-a-loo- ma's'.

Jack Frost

One thing we don't seem to see nowadays are the lovely patterns made by 'Jack Frost' on the windows in the winter. They were somewhat obscured during the war by the brown sticky paper criss-crossed on all the windows, this was to prevent injuries from flying glass during an air raid (and didn't the glue on the brown paper taste disgusting?). After the war, with the paper pulled off and the awful blackout curtains taken down, 'Jack Frost' could again be seen on cold winter mornings in all his glory. There was no central heating or double-glazing, and the bedroom floors were not carpeted, they were just covered in cold linoleum and the occasional rug.

A Christmas party

One Christmas eve the neighbour next to Mrs K (where Joy slept) asked Mrs L if I could baby-sit and stay the night. Permission was granted, but when I arrived it appeared a plan had been cooked up for me to go to a party. The two families had a hole in their dividing fence at the back of the houses through which I was gently pushed into the K's house. Mr K was in the Navy and had been on HMS. *King George V* throughout the war, he was now home on leave. Also at the party was Mrs K's brother, he'd just returned home after suffering a great deal, both physically and mentally, as a prisoner of war in Italy. I can remember being poured a 'Port and Lemon' to drink which I placed on the mantelpiece, it was like the magic porridge pot, no matter how often I drank from my glass … it remained full. The last thing I remember was dancing to a record called 'Forty Ginger Sailor Boys'. I was told the next day that as I stood against the wall my legs just buckled under me as I slowly sank to a crumpled heap on the floor. I do remember getting up next morning in the house I was supposed to be in, being very sick at six am. and trying to get dressed in time for seven o'clock communion.

Confirmation

I was confirmed at the age of thirteen by the Bishop of Salisbury at St. Mark's Church. I was dressed completely in white, dress, socks, shoes and a white veil to cover my hair. The actual service took place in St. Mark's Church on the other side of town as our local church was still a temporary building. We left our pews in pairs, one boy and one girl, and knelt in front of Bishop John of Salisbury. He said 'Bless this child' and placing his hand on my head I thought 'Ouch, that ring hurts', and it did! not a very Holy thought for the occasion. I could now take Communion, but pray as I might the situation at the L's did not improve.

Lack of domestic appliances

Before I go into details of everyday chores, it seems an appropriate time to mention the lack of domestic appliances that are now part of every housewife's kitchen. For instance, in the average working class household there was no washing machine, spin-dryer, dish-washer, refrigerator, micro-wave oven, telephone or television. To make a lather for washing-up, (soap was rationed) we would put a piece of green soap in a long-handled wire basket and beat it up and down in the water until bubbles appeared, a good method of using up all the 'bar-ends' of soap left over from washing the coloureds in the 'Butler' sink. Soap for laundry was a big green block of 'Fairy' and for toilet soap we used the red bars of carbolic soap, I can remember how lovely 'Lux' toilet soap smelt when we were able to buy it in the shops once the war had finished. Another thing that was out of production from 1939 to 1945 was paint and wallpaper, so when the war ended it was decided to decorate the dining-room. Mr L brought home some cream coloured distemper (which I thought was a disease caught by dogs!) and after it had been applied to the walls, some blue dye was added to the remainder. Each of us, holding a sponge, dabbed the walls to make an abstract pattern. I was informed it gave the impression of wallpaper, I wasn't convinced. It looked awful!

Monday – washing

Mondays were quite a ritual. The day would start with the lighting of the copper boiler. Washing had to be sorted into coloureds and whites, whites were put into the copper and pushed down into the boiling water with a dolly-stick (it resembled a big wooden pair of pliers, or those things used now-a-days to turn the sausages on the Barbie). The boiler was then left to boil for what seemed hours. When the 'whites' had boiled for the required length of time they were plunged into cold water that had been coloured blue with a 'Dolly-bag', and finally the linens, blouses, shirts and shirt collars were rinsed in starch before going through the mangle. It was all very laborious and time consuming. Coloureds were handwashed in the Butler sink and removing stains was a trifle hard on the knuckles; there were no synthetic fabrics and the woollen clothes had to be carefully squeezed by hand and took ages to dry. The whole of Monday was given over to laundry. There was no spin-drier and the clothes line was suspended on two high poles one at each end of the long garden; a prop was placed in the centre to avoid the sheets dragging in the dirt. The biggest nightmare was when the clothes line broke with the sheer weight of wet laundry blowing in the wind, and if the washing was still damp … the mud-spattered items had to be lifted off the ground, and the whole rigmarole was repeated from the beginning. Mr.L then walked into a tirade of abuse as soon as he came home from work to repair the line.

The iron mangle was kept in the garage, but every Monday morning it was lifted into the garden, all the clothes were fed through the rollers before being pegged out to dry. Putting the sheets through the mangle was left until I came home for lunch while at Junior School, and evenings when I attended Grammar School. It required one pair of hands to feed the sheets through the mangle and another pair to take them the other side. One lunchtime, as I was feeding the sheets into the mangle I let out an almighty yell, the second finger on my right hand was caught in the cogs and going round with each turn of the handle … and Mrs L was still turning! She quickly reversed the process to release my finger, but believe me it was just as painful being released as it was in getting trapped. Mr L, who'd heard the noise, came out to see what all the fuss was about. He led me indoors to bandage my finger; I then returned to school. I don't know how I concentrated on lessons that afternoon, the throbbing under the bandage was almost unbearable. The nail on that finger hasn't grown properly since, perhaps that's why.

Tuesday – ironing

Tuesday after school there was the pile of ironing to get through, drip-dry shirts were non-existent in the 1940s, the school blouses and boarders' shirts were all made of cotton and had been starched, so before they were ironed they were splashed with water and rolled into a tight roll to make them damp enough to iron … no steam-irons; it took two people to fold the sheets and pull them into shape. Mrs L would pull so hard at her end but woe-betide me if I dropped the sheet at my end … my right- her left- my right- her left etc, etc. Who needs aerobics? Tissues weren't in vogue so even handkerchiefs had to be ironed in their dozens, they had to be ironed properly, corners first before folding them into squares for the male handkerchiefs and neat little triangles for the ladies, it was a laborious job and very time consuming. After a day at school it was a long and tiring chore, working my way through the piles of ironing; no items were left for the following week, the laundry basket had to be cleared before bed-time on Tuesday night.

Some of the things I thought would be useful in later life didn't really turn out that way. For instance, I learnt to darn the men's socks and the awful thick orange stockings we wore to school. I would sit on a stool and place a wooden 'mushroom' under the hole to be mended, but if the finished result was not a perfect weave I would be punished, unpick my darning and start all over again, until it reached Mrs L's required standard. I could turn a sheet 'sides-to-middle'. This meant that the sheet was cut in half where the centre was thin and worn, the two halves with the outside edges were joined so that the thin parts of the sheet then became the outside edges. I could also neatly patch a hole. I learnt to knit; because of a shortage of clothes coupons we would unpick anything that was woollen and then re-knit the wool into a new striped jumper. Needle work lessons at school were also practical. We would make green check knickers for PT, or the blue aprons and pull-on sleeves that we wore for Biology, Chemistry, Physics and Art, but dressmaking was not my forte. I missed many a Friday's games lesson re-doing 'run-and-fell' seams, I just couldn't get them flat. The more they were unpicked the more frayed the material and the more difficult the task. Cooking was a more useful attribute. Food was rationed during the war and continued for several years after the war had ended, so cooking was primarily to learn to make tasty and nutritious food with whatever ingredients were available. We didn't have ready-made or frozen pastry and there were no packeted cake mixes, we learnt to make everything from scratch so to speak. In later years these lessons came in very useful. I think my family were amazed at how far a chicken would go and how little meat is needed to make a dozen Cornish Pasties!

When I was twelve years old Mrs L thought it would be a good idea if I had private piano tuition. I was hopeless at it. The money would have been better spent on Joy, she at least could play a tune by ear. There was a piece of music by Ezra Reed called 'Fire'; I would push down on the loud pedal and thump away as if my life depended on it. Mrs L would smile at her friends and say 'how lucky I was to be getting such expensive tuition'. I could also make an impressive noise playing arpeggios, again with my foot pressed hard on the loud pedal. I'm glad these visitors had no knowledge of music! The lessons however did serve a purpose, it meant I was out of the house two evenings a week. I had a boyfriend who would meet me on the way to lessons, wait for an hour and then walk me home again. He was also a morale booster, though unaware of this. I would be at home doing the endless chores in the evening, when suddenly there would be loud whistling and 'Tarzan' calls as he free-wheeled down the hill on his bicycle and past the house. Sometimes all his mates would join in. I would allow myself a secret smile, for it was very comforting to know that someone cared. I'm ashamed to say a lot of money was wasted trying to make me into a pianist. I had two teachers, one was the Music teacher at the Grammar School, Miss Walpole, and the other poor lady who lived nearby was supposed to teach me popular music. I remember playing 'Home Sweet Home' (my heart was not in the sentiments of that particular song) at Mrs L's request,

Darning, mending and making

Piano Lessons

making a hash of 'Bells across the meadow' and decimating 'The Blue Danube'. I was talentless! For some strange reason though, I was entered for an exam and I don't envy any aspiring young musician that experience. I walked into a very long room with a highly polished floor, a piano at one end and three Judges sitting miles away (well it seemed like miles to me). I did my stuff, so to speak and left. Unbelievably I passed, but I still can't play the piano. The limited knowledge I do have is useful when I try to solve crossword puzzles, but I haven't touched a keyboard since I was seventeen. I went to see a film in which Eileen Joyce played the 'Cornish Rhapsody' … I knew I would never ever reach her standard as a pianist, so I gave up!

Post-war fruit

My first memories once the war had ended, were not exactly good ones. Firstly Mr L bought home some pomegranates, the first imported fruit for five years. I thought they tasted fantastic, very sweet and juicy, but I must confess I made a pig of myself eating them. As a result I was extremely sick that night. As my bed was on the landing, I leave it to the imagination as to how far it spread and the amount of cleaning up it entailed. I repeated my greediness with a new jam called pineapple preserve, but in retrospect I think it contained more swede than fruit, and my digestive system didn't handle it very well, so back to cleaning up again. Needless to say I've never eaten a pomegranate or pineapple jam since! These two items of food couldn't quite compare with the 'meat substitute' which was the brain-wave of the Ministry of Food at the time … whale meat! It looked like beef and tasted of fish, it played hell with the eyes and taste-buds, expecting one thing and tasting something completely different. I think we all thought that food would be in plentiful supply now the hostilities had ended. Although bread coupons were no longer needed, clothes, coal and food were still tightly controlled. Rationing remained for another eight years.

The races

Mr L took me to Salisbury races, but to be honest I thought they were quite boring. The dog would enjoy the day out but there was a lot of waiting about between races. There was a very colourful character called Prince Honolulu (at least I think that's his correct name), he would sport an Indian Chief's headress and from shoulder to feet he was covered in a long, flowing red robe. 'I've got a horse, I've got a horse' he would cry.

He'd sell small slips of paper with a horse's name written on it for two shillings. I worked out that at least one buyer would be lucky, all the others would be 'also-rans'! I would accompany Mr L to Bournemouth to watch the 'Cherries' play football, and I enjoyed these days out as we usually ate at Beales and spent some time buying stamps for my collection before returning to Salisbury.

Boxing

As I mentioned earlier Mr L was a boxing fan and we tuned into the American radio broadcasts in the early hours of the morning. If my memory is correct about 4a.m., the reception was terrible with loads of static. One evening he said he had a surprise for me. We went to Victoria Park on the outskirts of

Salisbury, to watch a demonstration fight by the British heavyweight champi-
on, Freddie Mills. The ring was set on a platform in the open-air, enabling
everyone a ringside view of the proceedings. It was really an exciting evening,
I had previously only seen pictures of him in the *Daily Herald* or listened to the
fights on the radio, so it was a real treat to see him 'in the flesh' so to speak.

There were a number of Romany Gypsies living in the Salisbury area and
they would call on house-holders with their hand-made wooden pegs and
sprigs of 'lucky-heather'. Sometimes Mrs L would give them old clothes, they
were always most polite and respectful. I have a vivid memory of a Romany
funeral. The Market Square in Salisbury was a mass of black. I had never seen
anything like it before, or since for that matter. Young children wore black
shoes several sizes too big and even babies were swathed in black. Someone said
it was the death of the King of the Romanies but I don't really know for sure;
it was certainly a sight to behold.

Romanies

Joy had left school and was working in an office, she also had a boyfriend,
G. He would visit in the evening and then ride her bike to his home at Wilton,
returning it in time for her to use for work next morning. I didn't realise it was
serious until one day she said,

'All hell will break out on Friday, sorry'.

It appeared that every evening when G rode the cycle to his home it contained some of Joy's clothes in the basket and Thursday was the final trip. She
was going to stay with her boyfriend's Aunt until they married. Now – after
school on a Friday it was bedroom cleaning day. Cleaning was not a quick dust
and vacuum, nothing was that easy. I had to take everything out of the
wardrobe and drawers, move the heavy furniture to clean behind, even the
springs of the beds were dusted. When I thought I'd finished Mrs L would do
an inspection, fingers checking everything for just one speck of missed dust
and the inevitable thwack! ... hence Joy's warning about Friday! As I opened
the drawers and cupboards, they were absolutely empty! I carried on as normal, saying nothing and waiting for the inspection, but I must admit I was feeling a bit tense. I soon knew when the inspection started, there was an almighty
scream of rage followed by a very, very angry Mrs L. She looked as if she was
about to burst a blood-vessel, for the first time in her life she was completely
stunned. I'm just sorry Joy didn't see the bewildered expression on Mrs L's
face, it should have been recorded on film for prosperity (not that anyone
would want a photo of Mrs L). I was not quite sure how this would affect my
day-to-day existence, I would have to wait and see, but I was allowed to see
Bambi at the cinema and the song 'Love is a Song that Never Ends' seemed particularly poignant to me at that time. It was three years before I saw my sister
again.

**Friday – bedroom
cleaning**

**Joy drops a
bombshell**

Early on in the post war years, the Army would stage recruiting drives for
the various regiments. Every male had to do a minimum two years' National
Service and the regulars, who'd been fighting abroad for five years, couldn't

wait to be demobbed. They'd seen enough bloodshed to last them a life time, thus the Army had a shortfall of Regulars. The display I remember the best was put on by the 'Black Watch'; it was so colourful. Playing their bagpipes, kilts and sporrans swinging they marched and counter-marched on the market square. It brought back memories of Southsea Barracks, where as a child I'd watched the Highlanders march through the gates to war.

I'm not quite sure of the connection between Miss Kelly and the L's. I do know that my Mother worked for Miss Kelly in her sweet shop in Beamister Lane, Gosport during the late 1920s, before she married my Father. I also remember her visiting us at Larkhill, but I cannot find a link between Miss Kelly, my Mother and the L's, so I was very surprised when the L's said we were going to visit Miss Kelly in the workhouse. It was a large, red brick Victorian building on the outskirts of Salisbury, very stark and austere from the outside and pretty cheerless inside. We walked on bare wooden floors, the echo of our footsteps bounced off the walls as we made our way up a metal staircase to the women's' dormitory. On both sides of the room were rows of iron beds, standing to attention like soldiers on parade on the bare wooden floor. There were no bedside tables or anything that personalised one bed from the other, even the bed-spreads were uniformly matched. Throughout the building there was a strong smell of carbolic. Halfway down the room, lying in one of the beds was this little old lady I barely recognised. I do not know how her circumstances had changed for her to end up in the workhouse, nor do I know what became of her after our visit, I didn't go again.

The workhouse

Salisbury Fair

The big event each October in Salisbury, was the annual fair. All the streets surrounding the Market Square were closed to traffic and the centre of the City became one giant funfair. It appears that King Henry VIII gave Salisbury a special charter, so all the small fairs would congregate there at the end of the season before going to their winter quarters. It was a marvellous place to just wander around without spending any money and meet all your friends. It was so large it was like a big hiding place, never knowing who you would meet round the next corner. My favourite rides were the Carousel and the swingboats, the latter rising high above everyone's head so that I could gaze down on the crowds below. The newest ride was the 'Waltzer', it would go round and round in circles while the car would spin around at the same time. The best way to have extra excitement was on the 'Bumper-cars'. The boys would try to crash into the girl they wished to impress, as many times as possible in the short time allowed for each ride. Escapism at its very best! They also had boxing booths where the local lads could prove their masculinity, but they rarely won the prize money, it inevitably went to the resident pugilist. The rides seem tame compared to today's rides but I believe the thrills and enjoyment were just as great, and at least your legs still supported you when you were back on the ground!

The next big event after hostilities had ended in 1945 was the General Election. We'd had a coalition government during the war led by Winston Churchill and I think everyone believed Churchill would win hands down, he was the hero who saved us from the Nazis after all. Mr L was a staunch Labour supporter and strong trade-unionist. I helped him make a flag to put on the front of his car, it was red with a yellow hammer and sickle on it, I was quite proud of my handiwork. I was roped in to address the envelopes to be sent to every household in the district, a very fervent little leftist I was at that time. Churchill had not banked on the strength of the services wanting a change of government when they returned to civvy street and the Socialist Party led by Clement Attlee won the day. **General Election**

We had a series of second-hand cars; petrol could only be obtained with a special licence or on medical grounds, so there were plenty of cheap cars on the market. Mr L realised it was a good way to make extra money, buying and selling cars. My favourite was a maroon Lanchester, it was so comfortable to ride in, I was sorry to see it go. Mr L. had been promised by the local garage that he would have the first new car, whatever make, when the factories reverted to car production from munitions. It was a very proud day when he took delivery of a brand new Vauxhall 'Wyvern'. **A new car**

Woolworth's was the shop for spending one's pocket-money. We could buy sheet-music for sixpence and learn the words of the latest pop songs on the radio and yes, Jimmy Young was very popular in spite of Ken Bruce's remarks on Radio Two in the 'Eighties' and 'Nineties'! His version of 'Too Young' was very meaningful to teenagers falling in love. **Woolworth's**

To make our hair resemble, however slightly, the stars from Hollywood, we would buy metal 'Dinky' curlers and dampen our hair with sugar-water before rolling it up in them. Luckily I was too tired by bedtime to let their discomfort disturb my sleep. I would buy 'Gardinia' perfume by 'Goya', wear pink 'Cyclamen' lipstick by 'Outdoor Girl', use 'Pond's' vanishing cream before finally covering my face in thick, pancake makeup by 'Max Factor', and thinking I looked the 'bees-knees'. I was queuing to see a 'Doris Day' film one day and my 'date' went on and on about Doris's freckles and how lovely he thought they were. I could easily have screamed as I had hundreds of freckles covering my face beneath the thick layers of make-up! I'd been told as a very young child that the way to get rid of freckles was to wash the face in dew at 4a.m., I never tried it. **Make-up**

The next occupant of the front room was a lady hairdresser. She had the most beautiful deep auburn hair, long, wavy and thick. I was unaware at this **A new lodger** time that anyone could have their hair that colour with the help of Henna; needless to say I was a fervent admirer of hers. I was again sleeping on my wardrobe bed on the landing. I did have one very sticky moment when I was cleaning her room. She had statues of Saints, the Virgin Mary and a small bottle of fluid labelled 'Holy Water'. I was not well versed in the ways of Catholicism, so being nosy I unscrewed the bottle of water. The door suddenly opened and doing what I shouldn't, I nearly jumped out of my skin and spilt the water all over the carpet …. Fluffy walked through the door! I filled the bottle with water from the tap and no-one seemed any the wiser. One thing I did learn from this lady which was most useful;— when suede shoes are scuffed and tatty, polish them with shoe polish and they buff up like leather. As shoe buying was one of my *bete-noires* I was very grateful for this tip, leaving precious clothing coupons to be spent on something more urgent, like skirts and blouses. One evening the hairdresser managed to get permission for me to go out with her for the evening. We went to a dance at the George Hotel in Amesbury village and although this lady had fantastic hair, her figure was not too good. During the evening I was partnered by an Army Officer, who by any stretch of the imagination was too old for me but the right age for 'The Lady'. Her friendliness towards me as the evening wore on was getting decidedly chilly and she didn't invite me to accompany her again.

A perm!

Lodging with us in 1947 were two bus-conductresses, or 'clippies' as they were called. I became great friends with K, she had moved to the city from one of the surrounding villages and in her strong 'Moon-raker' accent she would call me Jonah. Wiltshire people are called Moonrakers. The story goes, 'Three yokels were going home very drunk one night, when they saw the moon's reflection in a pond, whereupon they tried to fish the moon out of the pond with fishing-nets'. K was like a breath of fresh air with her bubbly personality. She fell in love with her bus driver and when he proposed she asked if I could be her bridesmaid. Permission was granted. Extra excitement was caused when I was told I could have my first 'perm'; the magic of having curly hair everyday without putting in those dreadful curlers was good cause for excitement. There's nothing worse for straight hair artificially curled, than the damp atmosphere of the Avon valley, and whoever saw a screen-goddess with straight hair! It certainly was an experience not to be missed.

I was filled with excited anticipation as I sat in the salon chair. This was to be very different from the last trip to the hairdressers when I had that dreadful 'Eton-Crop'. My hair was divided into tufts which were pulled through rubber squares to protect my head from burns. A large machine was placed behind my chair and each clump was gripped by red-hot curlers from the contraption behind me, the smell of burning hair filled my nostrils and seemed to permeate the air in the salon, my head weighed a ton. I felt that this treatment was my first step to adult-hood. The bonus of these perms was that they stayed put! The only way not to have dry, frizzy hair was to wait for it to grow out or be cut, otherwise it stayed with you. I discovered that by using 'Kirby' grips to wind the hair while it was wet, would help to 'de-frizz' my tresses. K bought me a beautiful pale blue off the shoulder dress, it was long and full skirted. The whole day was wonderful. The Bride and Groom were happy, she looked radiant as only brides can look, the sun shone brightly and the family laughed and joked together. So much warmth and friendliness, it was a truly brilliant day.

Prior to Joy's escape we would go dancing on Saturday evenings in the village hall in Wilton. I think it was patronised by most youngsters in our age group and it became a popular meeting place. Live music was supplied by various groups, none well known, but it was always well played in strict tempo, the floor was a bit rough but nobody seem to notice. I recall one bandsman played the 'saw'. I don't know the techniques of this but it gave out a high-pitched whining sound and was certainly different! We didn't have to worry too much about money, the refreshments consisted of a rock-cake, a cup of tea or a glass of orange squash and on fine evenings we could walk the three or so miles back home. My hair was tightly plaited into two 'pigtails' before I left home, but as soon as I'd turned the corner of the road I would take them out, (not too disastrous as the plaiting at least made my hair wavy), only to have Joy re-plait my hair for me before returning home.

Hair has always been a problem with me, fine, mousy-coloured and dead straight (ideal for the 1990s but not in vogue in the 1940s). I longed to emulate the Stars of the Screen with their long, thick wavy hair. After the dreaded 'pig-tails' I tried the new American 'pony-tail' style, which was okay as long as I wanted to look young. Being female and seeing all those wonderfully sophisticated stars on the screen with their flowing tresses, I had to come up with something different. I decided on a 'page-boy bob'. I blame Veronica Lake and Lauren Bacall for this idea; it would be more manageable, or so I thought, as long as I could stand the torture of the 'Dinkey' curlers. There was no such thing as a hairspray and although sugar-water helped a bit, it was not conducive to having fingers run through one's tresses! During the day while I was working, there was the old stand-by, the hairnet, and travelling to and from work … the headscarf. I would leave my hair barely combed so as not to disturb the ends, but in the evening I would comb it right through, turn under the ends and Hey-Presto! a page-boy hairstyle. It looked so easy and worked well … as long as there was no wind, rain, fog or drizzle! Aunt May had a good way to style her hair for someone with little time, she would tie a shoe-lace around the top of her hair, fold the ends around the shoe-lace and that was that, neat, tidy and effective.

A good method of saving in those days was the sixpenny money-box. The circumference of the small tin was the size of a sixpence and tall enough to hold

Saving money

fifteen shillings exactly, when full the lid would pop off and you'd take your money to the Post Office to buy a Savings Certificate. These would increase in value depending on the length of time they were allowed to mature. I did own quite a few, but when I tried to cash them in several years later they had already been realised! I also saved a pound a week from my wages when I started work, but one day Mr L said he was behind with the rent (he'd lost it on the horses if the truth be known) and would I lend him £11. He accompanied me to the Post-Office and I gave him the money. Needless to say I never was re-paid!

Shorthand and typing

Mr L thought it would be a good idea for me to attend evening classes to learn shorthand and typing, so he registered me for night school at the local 'Pitman's' agency. I found it interesting at first, and of course there was the added bonus of escaping from the house for a couple of hours twice a week. Typing as many as forty words a minute with a cover over the keyboard was fine, but then it got complicated, margins, headings, and the dreaded short-hand. I could not understand all those squiggles and then read them back, a bit like trying to understand algebra or chemical symbols instead of their proper names. No! not my forte. Naturally I wasn't about to tell them at home that I was skipping lessons, there were more interesting things I could do to fill in this extra free time. I didn't take into account that the school would inform Mr L that I wasn't turning up for my lessons ... I was in deep trouble!

1947 – the big freeze

In the winter of 1947 it snowed and snowed and snowed. We thought we would never see green grass again, I think it was the longest winter on record. All football matches were cancelled and school was open to half its normal intake; the children in outlying districts couldn't get into the city, roads were blocked and many buses were cancelled. Personally I would have crawled through a blizzard rather than stay at home, although others were delighted by the extra 'holiday'. The thaw finally came in April and it was wonderful to see the green of the trees and grass again. Strange how you miss the colour when it's not there.

The milk-bar – my first job

My sixteenth birthday was in April 1949 and as the terms of Grammar School stated that you be educated until you reached sixteen years of age, Mrs L decided I leave school at Easter instead of staying to take the School Certifi-cate during the Summer Term. She found me a job in a new style milk-bar in the town, it was the first for Salisbury and was an American idea as a meeting place for teenagers. It had all the new-fangled coffee machines and the decor was a mass of chrome, formica and red plastic. When former school friends came into the cafe to be served I always found something urgent to do at the back of the cafe, I was so ashamed of the job I just had to hide. The good thing from my point of view was the long hours spent away from home, the opening hours were from early morning to late at night so I could work as long as I chose; there was no extra pay for the extra time worked, but I didn't mind so long as I was away from home. I would start at half seven in the morning and work through to the evening. I preferred twelve hours in pleasant company to working in fear of rebuke at home. My employers really took advantage of me, as I was a good and obliging member of staff and no matter how many hours I worked, the pay remained the same at £3 10s. a week. The job involved many things. I was expert at making sandwiches (plenty of practice at home), serving at the counter, washing-up (used to that) and on frosty mornings I even made soup with split peas and the skin and bone from the gammon ham; the market stall holders, who'd travelled in from the country at the crack of dawn, really appreciated this hot snack. It's amazing the amount of food we prepared in what was literally a small cubby-hole. There were our regulars, who'd arrive by bus from the various rural areas to attend the public and private schools which abounded in the city. We also had coach-parties which meant a hectic ten to fifteen minutes and then all quiet again. The busiest time though, was the summer. We had the new cold drinks machines installed and advertised the many ice-cream dishes from America, but because of shortages they were sold on Sunday afternoons only. It was a nightmare of continuous queues for ice-cream sundaes, knickerbocker glories, ice-cream sodas and Peach Melbas. I was becoming most proficient with these, and as we were so busy the time just sped by. I loved the continuous contact with people and the friendliness of everyone. The cafe had its own bakery and first thing every morning the baker would arrive carrying shoulder high trays of hot jam doughnuts, cream (synthetic only) doughnuts and crispy crescent rolls. Needless to say, I ate doughnuts and crusty crescent rolls layered in butter, heaven! The fancier cakes and freshly baked bread (unsliced) came later in the day. I filled the sandwiches with tinned salmon or freshly cut ham off the bone. After all the rationing it was wonderful to 'pig-out' on all this free food. (It's not surprising that I was a size sixteen). I was allowed a special concession on Sunday———yes, I did work a seven-day week. The cafe owner also owned a restaurant and I was allowed a free three-course meal, soup, roast and dessert, the feeling of being waited on was just wonderful! Mind you I needed a good meal inside me, as Sunday afternoon I had to cope with the endless demand for ice-cream. The queue would stretch halfway round the block, ice-cream was still a novelty as it hadn't been seen for so long.

Nylons

Similar excitement was generated with the appearance of bananas and citrus fruits. However, to the females the first buzz that nylon stockings were on sale in Style and Gerrish, the nearby department store, was really something. The boss allowed his staff to take turns to queue. The cost of one pair of nylons was 17/6d. As wages were only £3 10s. per week, and £1 30s. went to Mrs L for my keep, it was a lot of money. Again I found my height a disadvantage, the stockings were very short in the leg and to make them reach my suspenders I had to cut the double welt at the top of each stocking! The life-span of these nylons was brief, but a new industry was quickly set up in the windows of all the dry-cleaners, women could be seen huddled over a table invisibly mending the ladders.

Market day

I was becoming very adept at buying produce from the market. I would go to the stall-holders every Tuesday and Saturday to buy fresh produce to fill the cafe sandwiches. When I wanted tomatoes for instance, I would turn the boat (box) upside down to ensure the quality tomatoes went all the way to the bottom and not just on the top layer. It didn't take long before I was known and the trader would automatically open the 'boat' from the bottom without having to be asked.

I think it was when I was crossing the market square that I first became aware of my bust. I had a blue cotton T-shirt which was quite a tight fit and as I was making my way to a stall I heard several wolf whistles. My face turned scarlet as I blushed with embarrassment. I made certain that I never went across the square again without my overall tightly buttoned up. (What I'd give for a wolf whistle today! don't they say that youth is wasted on the young?)

Standing outside the cafe each day was a paper-seller. I think the best way to describe him is to say he resembled 'Benny' the character from 'Crossroads', he was not very old and well known to everyone. Even my boss was known to trust him enough to place bets on the horses for him and then allow him to collect the winnings; which on occasions was quite a wad of notes. However there was something that puzzled me, he disappeared every November and re-appeared the following March. I asked my boss where he went. 'He's homeless, so as soon as the cold weather sets in he throws a brick through a shop window, gets arrested, goes to jail for three months and in the Spring returns to work.' Seemed to make sense to me!

Tuesday was primarily a cattle market when the farmers would bring their cows and sheep to be auctioned. Saturday was for the country folk to sell their produce, but both days were extremely busy and well patronised. There was an elderly gentleman who visited the cafe regularly on market days and it became a bit embarrassing when he started to shower me with gifts he'd bought from the stalls. It started with armfuls of flowers and then earrings, brooches and necklaces, not expensive jewellery just pretty gew-gaws. The other girls would tease me mercilessly, but one of the older ladies quoted 'Better an old man's darling than a young man's fool' … very true!

The young lads had the burning desire to be the proud owner of a new racing-bike with gears and low handle-bars. They would do paper rounds or any other part-time job to save money for their coveted machine! On Sundays they would meet inside the cafe, drinking coffee and plan a route for the day ahead. Normally I was the only member of staff at work that early, but I certainly made friends with a lot of people. One Sunday no-one turned up for work until noon! during which time there had been the usual cyclists, three coach loads of day trippers as well as the regulars. I would serve everyone then go round the tables to collect the money, (the cash till was the other side of the counter) hurriedly clear the tables, make sandwiches to replace the ones sold, wash the dirty plates, cutlery and cups before repeating the process each time there was another rush of customers! It was hectic, but the atmosphere was so friendly and none of the customers cheated on the payment due. When the boss finally put in an appearance the first thing he did was check the money against the till-roll and said the till was short! During his accusations his brother arrived and was not at all pleased to learn that I was left to hold the fort on my own. After checking the till he pointed out that the till-roll hadn't been moved back to zero the previous night. When he was told to pay me a bonus for all my hard work and keeping the customers happy, I was given ten shillings from the till … not enough to buy a pair of nylons!

The boy's fashions were very fetching at this time. The American influence was beginning to seep through and they would wear dark brown trousers and long drape camel-coloured jackets, much sexier than corduroy trousers and regulation School Blazers! The best dressed lads, and the ones with the most money, were in the Merchant Navy. They would sign up for a voyage in Southampton docks, hopefully with the Cunard Line to South Africa. It was during their travels that they brought back with them the latest fashions, looking much smarter than the locals who'd had five years of austerity and still needed coupons for their clothes. The competition was slightly unfair as the Merchant Navy lads had plenty of money with which to show off, they'd use taxis to take their girls out and only sit in the front circle of the cinema, the 3/6d. seats! The one consolation for the local lads was that the ship would soon be whisking their rivals away again for six weeks, while they would still be around.

Boys' fashions

I spent a lot of time walking! If I managed to finish work early, the last thing I wanted to do was go home. I could take several different routes. In the summertime my favourite walk home was via the water meadows. I'd go into the Cathedral Close and head towards Harnham, then follow the path through the meadows, climbing over stiles and eventually coming out on the road nearest to where I lived. The distance was approximately five miles, but it was a heavenly place to forget your troubles and simply daydream. Sometimes it was very muddy, but I loved the sight of the Water Iris and Wild Daffodils; I'd peer into the water beneath the small wooden bridges, see the frog-spawn and minnows – it was a dreamers' paradise. I rarely met anyone else and I'd pretend it was my own piece of land. At other times I'd imagine we were over-run by Germans and I was carrying secret messages for Churchill. In the winter months, when it was cold and dark, I'd kill time just walking round and round the City; I never felt nervous and was never propositioned. I think, in retrospect, that the feeling of safety was partly due to the presence of the 'Red-Caps' (Military Policemen) marching in pairs round the town.

The water meadows

One summer evening I was walking slowly home when I was surrounded by three tall young men (snapped me out of my thoughts of spying). One was dark-haired, one blonde and the other mousy haired. They didn't say a word as they walked beside me for two miles but made strange signals to each other, it

An unusual friendship

seemed they had some sort of secret code with which to communicate, which I didn't understand. I was becoming a trifle uneasy, as half way home I passed a large mental hospital and I was afraid that maybe they were supposed to be inside! I stopped at the corner of my road and turned to them and said 'This is as far as I go, goodbye'. The blonde man then handed me a piece of paper on which he'd written 'We are deaf and dumb, can we see you again?'. The relief was overwhelming. A friendship grew between the deaf and dumb boys and myself. They taught me the sign alphabet and several signs so that we could communicate; although they were marvellous at lip-reading I didn't master the talent myself. I would accompany them to their club and as they were keen table-tennis players I would go along with them on away matches, to act as a sort of unofficial interpreter. The blonde boy was very skilled at boxing and when the fair was in Salisbury he could make some useful pocket-money in the boxing-booth. He became well known and as he couldn't hear the bell at the start and end of each round, the referee would tap him on the shoulder to let him know when to start and when to return to his corner. He was also an excellent dancer, this puzzled me as he always kept in strict tempo. He explained that he could feel the vibrations of the double-bass and drums through the soles of his feet. I'm afraid to say the friendship came to an abrupt end for two reasons. Firstly the Vicar at their club asked me to stop seeing them, as he thought it was unfair for a girl with all her faculties to be a rival to the handicapped girls at the club. Secondly, I received a marriage proposal. The signs for 'love' and to be a rival to them 'like' are very similar and I had been using the wrong sign. His distress was painful to see, a hard lesson for me to learn that 'a little knowledge is a dangerous thing', I wouldn't have hurt him intentionally. An unhappy and miserable outcome to what had been a happy and friendly relationship. All the Deaf and Dumb community were lovely people and it annoyed me that they were only offered low paid employment as council workers or cobblers, regardless of their intellect.

Clothes always a problem

One of the women I worked with gave me a blouse she had grown out of. It was bright red silk with a polo-neck fastened by a zip at the back of the neck. I thought it was beautiful, the colour was flattering to my fair hair and skin, so I was really looking forward to wearing it on my next date. When I arrived home I showed it to Mrs L. She took one look at it and ripped it from top to bottom before throwing it into the dustbin. At this time I had moved from sleeping on the landing to the canvas camp bed in the front room with Granny L. I wet the bed that night for the first time in my life. I told Mr L in the morning, he gave me a one pound note and said leave it to him. I don't know how he handled it but I didn't hear any more. I was desperately short of clothes at this time as they were still rationed and I didn't have many coupons, but to make matters worse, after my first week at work Mrs L destroyed my whole wardrobe ... Her reason? I was now working so I could buy my own. My wages were low and after Mrs L had taken half of it for my keep, there was very little left for clothes. I also tried to save one pound a week in the Post Office, but that came to an abrupt end when Mr L borrowed the rent money. I would walk to work to save on bus fares. I went into Richard Shops in Salisbury and they'd agree to reserve a dress or skirt for me, allowing me to pay so much a week or until I had the required number of coupons. My first purchase was a blue pleated 'Goray' skirt (even then I was a size 'sixteen'). I learnt early on that if I had one basic skirt I need only buy a selection of blouses and jumpers to give the impression I had a large wardrobe. This was proved one day on the bus home when an old school friend asked me how I managed to have so many clothes? The poor girl also suffered badly from teenage spots and asked which make-up I used, I told her 'Pond's Vanishing Cream' as it was cheap at the time. I hate to admit it, but the lack of spots was probably due to Mrs L's insistence that I drank the cabbage water each day before lunch ... how I hated that hot, green, bitter liquid before meals!

I decided I needed more money, but to do this I must change my job. I started from the centre of town going into all the factories and shops asking if there were any vacancies and how much they paid. I ended up at the Odeon Cinema near the railway station. The pay was slightly better and the working hours meant I would be out every evening, a lot of hours away from the house! It would only be an extra ten shillings a week, but at least that was more than I was getting at the milk bar and there was plenty of opportunity for promotion. The main reason for wanting to be out in the evenings was the fact that, although I was seventeen years old, working and paying towards my keep, I still had to be home by half past eight. This made it very difficult to have any kind of social life. I'm amazed when I think back how tolerant my dates were, I seldom saw a film to its conclusion and watched more 'B' movies than main features. There was the added problem that nothing was ever guaranteed. Mrs L would give permission for me to go out and then renege at the last minute, or it would be permission granted if it didn't rain! Many a time I would want to go out when the day started stormy and wet, but Granny L would say 'Rain

The Odeon

before seven – sun before eleven', sometimes she was right! Another time there would be no obvious reason to stay in and just as I was about to leave the house she would say: 'Where do you think you're going? I haven't said you can leave the house'. I would have to stay at home doing the never ending chores instead of meeting my date.

The job at the Odeon opened a completely new way of life for me. The cinema doors would open to the public at half-past one, but I would arrive about half twelve and either go to 'Tony's' cafe or the 'Yorkshire Fisheries' for something to eat. Before we started our duty each day, there was a parade; the manager would inspect our wine-coloured jackets edged with gold braid and our plain wine skirts, see that our stockings weren't laddered and that the seams were straight, check our torches worked properly and didn't need new batteries, even our finger nails were inspected to make sure they were clean. Everything about the Cinema gave out an aura of luxury, except perhaps the cheapest seats at the front (9d.). A uniformed doorman would strut up and down the foyer to keep an eye on the continuous queues. A trip to the cinema was, after all, the family's weekly outing and people always dressed in their best clothes to see the latest film. I think I will remember the film shown during my first week at the cinema for the rest of my life, it was *Geronimo* and by the sixth day

The Newsreel

I knew the script by heart! The Newsreel was shared with the Gaumont Cinema; a boy would cycle between the two theatres carrying the film cans on his bike. As both cinemas were run by the Rank organisation it saved on costs. There was a third cinema in Salisbury called the Regal, they specifically showed all the M.G.M. (Metro, Goldwyn and Mayer) musicals. We would have a free pass to see the films at the Gaumont, but had to pay when we went to the Regal. There was a short period, in the late 1940s, when the Gaumont Cinema would put

Usherette

on Big Band shows on a Sunday afternoon (the law dictated that films were not allowed to start before four o'clock on Sunday afternoons). I saw bands such as Ted Heath and Oscar Rabin, with singers Denis Lotis and Eve Boswell, really excellent performances. Saturday mornings were for the children and I can only describe it as 'all hell let loose'. They would see their screen heroes such as Roy Rogers, Hop Along Cassidy and the eternal favourites Buck Rogers and Flash Gordon. We also screened old Charlie Chaplin silent films and cartoon films of Bugs Bunny, Mickey Mouse and Donald Duck.

The usherettes had a brief moment of stardom twice a day. As they stood at the front of the stage waiting for the lights to go on during the interval, loaded down with a tray of ice-cream suspended from a strap round their necks, the projectionist would pick them out in a spotlight. It inevitably gave rise to 'wolf-whistles' from the stalls ... I think maybe that was my fifteen minutes of fame.

Cashier

After a short spell as an usherette I was promoted to the box-office as cashier, it was the best job ever! Every Monday afternoon I would sit in the front circle to watch the new programme, this was to enable me to answer any queries that might be asked by the paying public about the film showing that week ... and I was getting paid to do it! I was relieved I was on my own when watching Bud Abbot and Lou Costello films. I laughed so much at their antics, I would hold my sides until they ached as I rolled about in my seat and banged the barrier of the front circle unable to contain myself, not behaviour to be witnessed, they were my favourite 'double act'. One film which I found very frightening was *The Picture of Dorian Grey* starring the extremely handsome Hurd Hatfield (whatever happened to him?), the gradual distortion of his portrait after he'd traded his soul to the Devil was cleverly done. The final scene when all his misdeeds were shown on the face of the picture was awesome! A crazy lady in the films of the 1940s was Carmen Miranda. She was South American and always looked the same which-ever film she was in, wore a sarong draped across her hips, a large and colourful frilly blouse and topped it all off with a ridiculous head-dress. Remembering that tropical fruit was something we didn't see, let alone eat, her head-gear could only be marvelled at, bananas, pineapples, apples, pears and fruit I'd never heard of, piled high upon her head! How she managed to balance this creation on her head while wiggling her hips and singing, is a mystery to me. I associate her with only one song, although I expect she sang others, it went 'Ay ay ay ay ay ay like you very much, ay ay ay ay ay ay think you're grand,' in a strong South American accent.

I didn't have to wear the uniform any more and it seemed at the time that everyone in Salisbury knew me. This was not surprising really, as the queues sometimes lasted for three hours with only the box-office and the walls to stare at! I remember one boyfriend became very quiet on the walk home from the cinema, and when I asked what was wrong, he said, 'I've counted that at least forty males have said "hello" to you on the way home.'

It was useless trying to explain that I didn't know any of them, but if someone says 'hello' to me, I naturally answer. The main feature started about eight in the evening and the cashing up was completed by half an hour later, technically I was free to go home, but at home they thought I worked until closing time. I had the feeling of a prisoner let out on parole, free but not quite. I was determined I would make the best of this bonus free time.

I would like to say that working in the box-office was not solely to sell the tickets. I was also responsible for doing the book-keeping. There were no calculators, I just had a ready-reckoner to assist me, so although I could check the price of say, three hundred at 1/9d., the columns of figures still had to tally with the number of tickets sold and monies taken at the close of each days' business. I became quite adept at adding up, but nowadays I'm numerically lazy and find it an effort to sort out the maths on *Countdown*.

Salisbury was an Army town so naturally I met a lot of young soldiers doing their National Service. The place to go for an inexpensive evening out, good company and dancing was the NAAFI club. Females could only be admitted if they were accompanied by a member of the Services, but for me this wasn't a problem. When a soldier visited the cinema with his girlfriend he wanted a back seat to canoodle with his date. Who better to use her influence than the cashier? In return I just had to make my way to the 'Club', along would come a familiar face and in we'd go. I think it's called 'You scratch my back, and I'll scratch yours.' Whatever … it was a good arrangement. The dancing was excellent, the army musicians would play strict tempo music and I soon learnt that

NAAFI club

dancing was something I enjoyed, and it was a wonderful form of escapism. It was an era when it was deemed rude for a female to refuse a dance when asked, the girls would sit on chairs surrounding the dance floor and … wait! I knew I was in for trouble when a male of, shall we say lesser stature, started to make his way to my chair. I would stand up, all five feet nine inches of me and look at my five feet four partner-to-be and ask 'Are you sure?'. One partner lifted my elbows in the air and used the space between to see where he was going, all good fun! There was a nice gesture from a male when dancing, he would place a handkerchief in his hand to prevent sweat marking his partner's dress or blouse, it seems quaint today, but it makes sense really! I spent a lot of time dancing without shoes, which ruined many a pair of stockings, but brought me down in size! I had to make sure I was back at the Odeon by closing time as every so often, especially if it was raining, Mr L would decide to give me a lift home. However, I always managed to be outside the cinema on time and didn't get caught out.

As I mentioned earlier there were two places opposite the Cinema where we would go to eat during our breaks and before starting work. One was the 'Yorkshire Fisheries', the best fish and chips in the world. I called the owner Uncle Jack because when Pop Bulford was alive he worked there; he peeled the potatoes and made the batter. Pop would have a large pail full of batter and with his massive fists he would beat the mixture (no electric mixers). The result was the lightest, crispiest batter I've ever tasted! Uncle Jack would save all the crispy bits for me and sprinkle them over my chips, he never charged me for my pennyworth of chips and fourpenny piece of cod. Another advantage of knowing the owner was that I never had to queue, I would go straight to the room at the back of the shop and be served in there, allowing me to eat my lunch at a table. The alternative was to eat with my fingers from the newspaper-wrapped food while walking along the street.

The other 'eating-hole' was 'Tony's', the owner was Italian and the girls from the Cinema became regular customers. He made delicious sandwiches and coffee, but the main attraction was his record-player! Now this was a rare thing in the early 1950s and he would play his records of Frankie Laine singing *Jealousy* at full volume, followed by *Ghost Riders in the Sky* … magic!

I had some memorable moments at the Odeon. For instance, the main film had started one afternoon and business was slow, when a patron asked for a three and sixpenny ticket for the front circle. I didn't take much notice except to hope that no one would sit behind her, as her large hat would obscure their view. I also thought it a bit strange that she wore dark glasses indoors. Five minutes later the manager came from his office looking decidedly flustered, he asked me,

'Do you know who you've sold a ticket to?'

I hadn't a clue. It was Greta Garbo. Her ticket money was promptly refunded, while I was sent post-haste across the road to 'Tony's' to buy sandwiches and

Yorkshire Fisheries

Tony's

Greta Garbo

coffee, the flustered Manager then proceeded to carry the tray upstairs to his honoured patron. I seem to recall reading somewhere that Miss Garbo frequently stayed with friends in Wiltshire.

Another event that stayed in my mind was the Premier of the *The Browning Version*, we didn't screen it until the days' programme had finished and several stars were expected to arrive as promotional guests. I was hoping to meet Jean Kent but she didn't arrive, however Wilfred Hyde White did. The girl who volunteered to do 'cloaks' said she nearly dropped his Astrakhan coat, it was so heavy, and instead of a normal coat-loop to hang it up by, it had a chain! She also bragged about the 10/- note he gave her as a tip.

The Rank organisation was very impressed with our turnover for the film *Alice in Wonderland*. We had non-stop queues from first performance to last, people thought nothing of queuing for three hours to see this latest Disney block-buster. All the staff were given a bonus of 10/- to show the management's appreciation of the high box-office takings for that week. Another record breaking film was *Harvey*. The manager took individual photos of each member of staff and pasted the life-size pictures onto a large frame, this was placed in the foyer next to a large card-board cut-out of 'Harvey', the big white rabbit! It was a lovely, gentle film with the actor James Stewart at his best. The most watched film by me was *Pandora and the Flying Dutchman*. Not only did it star James Mason and Ava Gardner, but it was a story that said you give up everything for love. To an impressionable seventeen year old it definitely had the 'aaaaghh' factor.

A news item that brought me to tears was the funeral of Ivor Novello. I was already a fan of his music (it reminded me of my last night at Summer School) and when I saw his coffin draped in Lilacs and the sound of his music *We'll Gather Lilacs* being played as the Funeral Cortege made its way through the streets … it was just too emotional for words!

I had a terrible crush on Alan Ladd, good-looking and blonde, always playing 'Mr. Nice-Guy' on the screen, but I'm ashamed to admit my adoration was short lived when I read in a magazine that he had to stand on a box to kiss his leading-ladies! I promptly switched my fickle heart to Gregory Peck, tall, dark and handsome, the exact opposite to the previous object of my desire. I was still undecided though, as the voice of James Mason and the looks of Dirk Bogard caused many a missed heartbeat! Watching so many 'B' movies, I became a fan of the actor Sidney Taffler: I don't know what became of him but he seemed to make a good living from minor films, usually as a 'baddie'.

We had a 'Boots the Chemist' opposite the Cinema and I would go there to **Boots** buy my cosmetics and perfume. I mentioned earlier that I used 'Pond's Vanishing Cream' as a base for my loose powder but I also bought 'Phul Nana' perfume to dab behind my ears, supposedly to give me an air of mystery, the bottle had an Eastern look to it and made one feel exotic. 'Soir-de-Paris' perfume was more expensive, but the dark blue bottle was in the shape of a miniature Eiffel

Tower ... *tres française*! A common sight in the Ladies' cloakrooms was to see the females spitting on a small black brush, rubbing it furiously on a cake of mascara and brushing their eyelashes with it (it's much easier these days ... just remove the wand and apply). After the de-rationing of soap, 'Boots' sold their own brand that was highly perfumed; my favourite was the yellow 'Jasmine' scented bar. I'd use it to wash during my tea-breaks and before leaving for the NAAFI club dance. I received many compliments on my choice of perfume, so I stopped buying the expensive essences and stuck to my soap. I suffered a lot at this time with bad headaches (can't think why) and the doorman would go across the road to 'Boots' where, for sixpence, they would mix me a headache draft. I never found out what it consisted of ... but it worked.

General Election 1957

The next General Election was whilst I was working in the cinema in 1951. This time it seemed more exciting, although I was still too young to vote (you had to be twenty-one years old). Televisions were still a rarity for the average household, so the Cinema had permission to stay open all night to flash up the results on the screen as they were announced. I'd told the L's that I had to work as it was a special event and all the staff had to stay behind, not true, but there was no argument. A large group of Army Officers sat in the Front Circle and we'd brought in sandwiches and cups of coffee (good old Tony) for refreshments to keep us going through the long night while we waited for each result to come in. Every time there was a Labour win a huge cheer would resound round the theatre ... great stuff! This time, however, after only one spell as Prime Minister, Mr Attlee was beaten and Winston Churchill again took over as leader of Britain.

Jazz Club

Another way the Army influenced my recreation time was the Jazz Club run by a group of military bandsmen in their off-duty time. They booked a room at the White Hart Hotel and called it 'The Blue Room,' their signature tune was 'Blue Moon' played on the xylophone, and we would meet every Tuesday evening. I was really developing an education in all types of music and I cannot stress enough how professional these army musicians were, whether they played marches, ballroom or jazz, they were excellent.

I was becoming very fashion conscious, which was not easy with the limited number of coupons each person was allotted, a shortage of cash and long legs that still made it impossible to get 'The Dior Look' just right. I do remember having a light grey whipcord coat, a grey 'Beanie' hat, maroon Moccasin- style shoes and gloves, I thought it looked very smart. The 'Beanie' was a hat that had taken off among the youngsters of America, it was a corduroy skull cap with a roll of corduroy surrounding it and it was worn on the back of the head. This was a huge improvement on the turbans and head-scarves most women had worn to cover their heads and protect their hair during the war years. There were, however some very inventive designs for the head-squares, I remember that I wore one with a large picture of Churchill in the centre and his war-time speeches printed around the border, very patriotic. There was no such thing as a 'Teenager' this is a term that was introduced much later, we were just 'in-betweens', that is, between leaving school and getting married. I don't honestly believe that females were expected to attain very much, just be eternally grateful if they found a good husband, preferably one who could keep you financially secure, otherwise you'd have to find 'a little job' to help out with housekeeping. We didn't have the status accorded to youngsters from the 1960s onwards, and the freedom of choice and status given to 1990s girls wasn't even considered a possibility!

I was very fortunate to see an exhibition of Van Gogh paintings in the Salisbury Guildhall. I was immediately taken with his 'Sunflowers' and the brightness of the yellow paint as he tried to capture the sunlight in his work. I was equally touched by the 'Potato Eaters', the darkness in contrast to his other works depicted the poverty of the peasants, making me feel so sad. His 'Self-portrait' showed his mental turmoil in the eyes and a lone chair in his room looked more like a prison cell to me. I know this is not how 'art experts' view the paintings of Van Gogh, but as a young girl it's how I remember them.

Art exhibition

I was doubly fortunate to live so near to the magnificent Gothic Cathedral. I would spend many hours just wandering around the Cloisters, in the Chapter House or just marvelling at the architecture. The black marble pillars in the nave seemed to be straining to keep the whole structure from collapsing, the slightly crooked spire, which was added to the tower as an after thought, reaching majestically four hundred and four feet into the sky, making it a welcome sight to anyone travelling home, for the spire could be seen in the distance long before you reached the outskirts of the City. I often stood by the big iron clock trying to fathom out how it worked and told the time, but the mystery always eluded me. I would make my way up to the tower, try to read the Magna Carta (my Latin was not that good) and look at the huge Bible secured by a chain on a lectern. The chain seemed superfluous to me, I couldn't imagine anyone being able to carry it from the tower let alone out of the Cathedral. The cloisters and chapter house were areas of tranquillity where I could just wander and reflect on my life. The Close and its surrounding areas were very peaceful and further across the fields, I could stand on the bridge to gaze at the same view of the Cathedral that John Constable had used for his painting a century before. It truly is a very beautiful city. I just regret that all my memories there are not happy ones.

Salisbury Cathedral

Learning about relationships was proving to be more difficult than I thought they should be as an 'in-betweenie'. When I worked in the cafe I was friendly with a boy from one of the local private schools, it was all very naïve and innocent. It consisted of hand holding, walks in the Close and sharing a cup of coffee or two. Imagine my surprise when I arrived home one day to find Mrs L had received a visit from this boy's mother forbidding me to see her precious son. She didn't approve of a 'cafe-worker' mixing with her well brought up child. ... She was a housekeeper! My first experience of being judged by surroundings and appearance and not as an individual.

Cadena Cafe

On weekday afternoons, the Cadena Cafe opposite the Market Square would have 'Tea-Dances' and as my hours of work were not known at home, I would go for tea and cakes (and there was nothing more tempting than a trolley of Cadena Cakes). Cakes during the war were a bit of a mine-field, just as you took a big bite … ugh, a mouthful of bi-carbonate of soda! I enjoyed watching the dancers, but the trouble with these groups was they'd all been to Modern Ballroom lessons at the same school. I'd watch them dancing in perfect tempo, going round and round in circles with nothing individual in their interpretation of the music. They looked like a group of marionettes with an unseen hand pulling their strings. Another attraction at the Cafe was the String Quartet that played while the customers enjoyed their tea and cakes. It seemed quite 'posh' although the music reminded me of school. Miss Walpole had been an excellent Music teacher, opening our minds to all kinds of music and performances. Various groups were invited to the school to educate us in the many different sounds of music, quartets, quintets and string trios. We had a lady guest one afternoon who demonstrated dance from all over the world, I think my favourite was when she donned red boots and a fur hat to demonstrate Cossack dancing. Great stuff! We tried to emulate the Cossack dance during our lunch breaks, squatting down with our arms folded across our chests, and attempting to shift our weight from one leg to the other, but it's harder than it looks, and most of us ended up flat on our backs in a giggling heap on the grass. Off on a tangent again, Joan!

Romantic young soldiers

A further worry with regard to relationships was with the National Servicemen. They were aged between eighteen and twenty-one and away from home for the first time in their young lives, they thought they'd fallen in love at the drop of a hat. I actually had nine proposals in the cinema from young servicemen. It was always during a particularly romantic scene, just as the hero and heroine were about to kiss, my date would pull me close and whisper in my ear, 'Will you marry me?'.

I thought at first that they were taking the 'mickey', as I was continually subjected to personal abuse and insults at home I hardly thought of myself as some sort of 'femme-fatal'. I certainly didn't consider myself capable of attracting a lover, never mind a marriage proposal! I was also afraid to hurt their feelings, so I always said 'Yes', then they would leave Salisbury and go back to their homes or be posted abroad. I would receive letters with 'BOLTOP' (Better On Lips Than On Paper) or 'SWALK' (Sealed With A Loving Kiss) written on the back of an envelope, a very risque 'BURMA' (Be Upstairs And Ready My Angel) did not receive a reply! I bet the postman had a few laughs during his round! I was continually amazed at the illiteracy of some of the letters and after a couple of badly written letters it would all fizzle out.

I did fall in love; it was totally unexpected and an emotion that completely overwhelmed me. He came from London and was doing his National Service with only a few months left to serve when we met. On my seventeenth birthday he bought me a lovely pink pendant and we went to the Regal Cinema to see the film *Three Little Words*. On the way home he said: 'Three little words mean I love you'.

I was elated ... over the moon ... on cloud nine ... or any other adjective that can even attempt to express the feelings of one's first awakening to love. As I was only seventeen years old we both knew we'd have to wait until I was twenty-one before we could marry. It didn't matter, as long engagements were the norm rather than the exception in 1950. For the first time in nearly ten years I found a reason for living and a happy ending on the horizon. I'd also applied at this time to St Thomas's Hospital in London to train as a nurse, this had long been an ambition of mine. It started when my Father gave me a wooden-jointed doll and a copy of *St. Johns hand-book on First-Aid*. I'd spent many happy hours practising my bandages on this doll, I would have preferred people but my brothers were less receptive! If I was accepted at St Thomas's I could fulfil a life-time ambition to go into nursing and also be near my boyfriend in London. Life had taken on a completely new meaning and for the first time I felt optimistic about my future. On the eve of his demob.(demobilisation) there was a farewell party at the NAAFI Club (where else!) and at the end of the evening the lads insisted on a kiss goodbye. They formed an orderly queue insisting that each would have a farewell kiss. I wondered why there were so many of them, then the penny finally dropped when I realised they were having a kiss and going back to the end of the queue for 'seconds' ... all good fun! The next day I went to the station and waved 'Goodbye' not realising I'd never see him again. He did write frequently and his letters were loving and caring, but I forgot the way Mrs L's mind worked. I was getting ready for work one morning when I heard Mrs L dictating a letter to one of her cronies. The letter was to be sent to my boyfriends' father saying that 'his son was going out with a prostitute and were they aware of their son's liaison.' I was horrified. He was an only child and for his family to receive such a letter was unthinkable, so I wrote him a letter telling him I didn't want him to write to me again and the relationship was over. It was the most painful thing I'd ever done. I didn't receive a reply. I cried more than I thought it was humanly possible, to say I was heart-broken would not fully describe the pain I was feeling; I was amazed at the amount of fluid stored in lachrymal ducts. His favourite song was Guy Mitchell singing *Sparrow in the Treetops* and each time I heard it played on the radio the 'water-works' would start all over again. One popular song at the time, which really tore me apart, was 'Once in a while, will you try to spare one little thought for me?'. I received an application form from St Thomas's Hospital but the L's refused to sign their consent for me to live in London, as I was under eighteen I needed my parents consent to live away from home. I was at a very low ebb.

Deception and despair

After the incident with the housekeeper's son, when I have to admit my pride was sorely wounded, I decided all men were equal. I wasn't bothered

An Army officer

whether my date was a Private or an Officer, blue collar worker or a professional, to me they were just males of the species. However, one suitor is worth
a mention. He was a Captain in the Artillery and we met through the box-office
(where I met most people). He asked me if I would like to go with him to see
a film at the Gaumont. I said 'Yes'. This was quite a different routine from the
usual date, queue for film, see film, eat ice-cream in the interval and walk
home. We started in a restaurant, I can't honestly say that I'd had a lot of experience eating out so to speak, and the times when I had, it was usually a meat
and two veg sort of menu. I was a trifle unsure what to do when I had to turn
over a piece of plaice and what one did with the slice of lemon. I followed his
lead with the lemon, but once I had eaten all the flesh on one side of the fish I
wondered how to turn it over. I think he sensed my predicament and I watched
as he slid the knife under his fish, fork on top and deftly flipped it over. When
it was time for the dessert, he clicked his fingers and called 'Old woman' to get
the waitress's attention. She was about forty years old! I remonstrated with
him, but he said all women in his country were old at forty! Arriving at the cinema in time for the main feature only, he bought chocolates, nuts, orange
drinks and ice-cream; my lap was piled high with 'goodies', there was enough
to feed an army, it was an eye-opening experience. (Note – there wasn't a drop
of alcohol throughout the whole evening.) We'd only had a few dates and his
behaviour towards me was impeccable at all times, not even an attempt at a
kiss, so imagine my surprise when he asked me to marry him and return with
him to live in India! He explained that with my fair hair and blue eyes I would
be much respected, but there was a catch … he was allowed four wives! He
explained, 'If I produced a son my permission would be required for subsequent wives, however, if I bore only female children, no permission from me
would be necessary, but I would always keep the status of 'Number One wife'
and control the household'. At seventeen years of age this did not seem a very
good offer. In retrospect I think I should have accepted.

**Sisters but
strangers**

I'd heard that my sister had married. I was forbidden to attend her wedding.
She had applied to the Court for permission to marry and to rub the L's noses
in it good and proper, she'd employed the same solicitor used by the prosecu-
tion when Mr L lost his job. Joy was eighteen years old but parents' permission
was required by Law if you were under twenty-one. The lady in whose house
Joy had slept for nine years lent her a wedding dress, and their daughter was
the Bridesmaid. It seems odd that we both lived in the same town but our paths
never crossed, we were sisters who were relative strangers to each other. We'd
been so successfully estranged by the L's that the thought of seeking out each
other's company didn't occur to either of us.

**Festival of Briain
1951**

In the summer of 1951 came the much heralded Festival of Britain. After
the austerity of the war years it was causing a great deal of excitement, there
was a general atmosphere of optimism in the Country. Hitler was dead, the
fighting was over, the Japanese were defeated and we were free and safe. Mr L

said he would take me to London to see the Festival. I had a new blue and white cotton dress that I'd bought from my favourite shop, Richards, it cost me the princely sum of four pounds (a whole week's wages) and most of my precious clothes coupons. I was really looking forward to a day out in London. Secretly, I was hoping to see my ex-boyfriend, which was a bit naïve really considering the size of London. I'm ashamed to say that the things I remember about the Festival are not about the fantastic achievements of British industry. If I'd had a crystal ball to see that I might one day try to write about events in the 1940s and 1950s, I would have been more observant. The first thing I recall is the long queue to get in, it snaked its way along the side of green railings for what seemed like miles, but the weather was hot and sunny and the atmosphere was one of anticipation. No one seemed to mind. I do of course remember the Battersea Fun-Fair, but the prices of the rides were prohibitive, unlike the sixpenny rides I was used to at Salisbury Fair. Even a simple thing like buying an ice-cream was quadruple the price I paid at home. I did enjoy the sail down the Thames and seeing Greenwich Palace, especially as there were no signs of the dreaded sea-sickness I'd suffered in Devon – I know it's a river and not the sea, but a boat is a boat is a boat as far as my psyche is concerned! Maybe the day out would have been less enjoyable if it had poured with rain or there had been thunderstorms and high winds, but this was an old fashioned summer's day with blue skies and brilliant sunshine.

I still had my phobia about buying shoes and when Mr L suggested he'd take me to a shoe shop in Oxford Street my heart sank … I was about to say into my boots but that seems a little inappropriate when about to enter a shoe shop! When the assistant asked me my shoe size I whispered 'eight' then held my breath as I waited for directions to the men's department. She just smiled and walked away and to my utter amazement she returned with at least half a dozen pairs of shoes in the dreaded size eight for me to try on. She sensed my surprise (perhaps she tripped over my jaw lying on the carpeted floor), so I explained my previous problem in the local shops. She laughed and said: 'Ladies with really big feet go into the basement, where we stock sizes nine to twelve'. In spite of all that reassurance I still don't like shoe shops, but it was a good day out. I also had two pairs of shoes that were both fashionable and comfortable … bliss!

Things finally came to a head! It was 18th December 1951. I was getting ready to go to work at lunch-time when Mrs L decided she would empty my handbag onto the table to see what it contained, I knew she did this from time to time but that particular morning I wasn't prepared. I had a ten-pack of Player's cigarettes in my bag and she went ballistic when she found them, I was seventeen and three quarters. She flew at my head, knocking me off my feet with the force of the blow. I rose to my feet, and with my head reeling I picked up my bag and left, supposedly to go to work. I went to the local playground where I sat crying for a while on the swings trying to collect my thoughts. Luckily it was a schoolday and no one else was in sight. I decided there and then

Leaving Salisbury

that I wouldn't return to the L's but would try to find my Mother. I didn't want to be brought back again, as had happened on my last futile attempt to leave the L's, so I decided to see Mr. Braggar the NSPCC Inspector and find out exactly how I stood legally if I left the L's. To my utter dismay he told me I could have left when I was sixteen and not be made to return … twenty-one months ago! My next port of call was the Manager of the Odeon, he was most understanding and kind, he wrote me a glowing reference and wished me 'Good Luck' as he shook my hand. I said my 'Good-byes' to the rest of the girls, feeling sad at leaving them all behind, as we'd had some great laughs together and had become good friends.

Aunt May with my cousins. She became Mayor of Blandford and was an important and hardworking person there

PART THREE

1950–53

I CROSSED THE ROAD OUTSIDE THE CINEMA AND SLOWLY MADE MY WAY to the railway station. I bought a ticket for the next train to Portsmouth. I don't precisely know why, except that subconsciously maybe it was the right direction to take. I hoped that my Grandmother Russell was still alive and living in the same house in Gosport that I remembered from my childhood, but perhaps most important of all, that she knew the whereabouts of my Mother. During the one hour journey I let my thoughts drift to the many times I had cried myself to sleep, imagining my Mother as an angel perched high on a pedestal, missing me as much as I missed her and her not knowing how to get in touch with me. I refused to believe in my heart the terrible things Mrs L had said about me being unwanted and given away, I somehow couldn't take on board the criticism about my parents. I would let the words wash over me, not wanting to hear them. I then tried to remember the way to my Grandmother's house once the train had pulled into the Harbour Station at Portsmouth. The fact that I only had what I stood up in, not even a change of underwear, didn't seem to be a problem. I only had enough money to buy my ticket as my Post Office savings had been spent by Mr L, but I firmly believed all these things would be alright once I found my family again … ah, the optimism of youth! An hour after boarding the train I was in Portsmouth. If I said I was calm and

Going to Portsmouth

collected it would be a lie. I was very afraid. I bought a one penny ticket for the ferry-boat which plied back and forth across the harbour, alighted at Gosport Haid, walked up the High Street and into Beaminster's Lane; so far so good, my memory was serving me well. I walked past Trinity Church towards Pneumonia Bridge and there it was … Sweets place.

Feeling very nervous I knocked on the door of number

four. The door opened and there stood my Grandmother, looking not a day older than my last memory of her. She said my name, then hugged me hard before she burst into tears. I'd almost forgotten how wonderful it felt to be hugged, I was back where I belonged. First things first, Gran put the kettle on to make a cup of tea, it was as if I had only seen her yesterday and not ten years before; I was a mere child of eight years old when we last saw each other and here I was a young woman almost eighteen years old. I asked her if she knew where my Mother lived and she assured me we would walk to her house as soon as I'd finished my tea. I think she needed a cup of tea to regain her own equilibrium before we walked to my Mother's home.

Finding Mother and brothers

We chatted as we made our way past Walpole Park, along Stoke Road and finally turned a corner towards Gosport Park. We reached a prefab. (prefabricated house) estate on the edge of town. Gran knocked on the door and when it opened, not only was my Mother there but also my two brothers. My elder brother was wearing the uniform of the RAF and my younger brother was in the cadet uniform of the Merchant Navy. I was in too much of a daze to notice the coldness of my Mother's welcome, but my brothers' joy was overwhelming. One on either side of me they wrapped me in their arms in a bear hug. I felt safe for the first time since 1941. At last I was back home. It was just a week to Christmas 1951. Mum was worried the council would charge her extra rent as I would be classed as a lodger. No-one knew she had daughters, on the Council forms she only had two sons. There was the added problem of having no clothes with me, this was overcome a little by a friendly neighbour who gave me underwear as an early Christmas present. Mum took me to C&A at Portsmouth to buy a coat, it was green with a tie-belt and cost £4; I was to repay my Mother as soon as I had a job. On the second evening of my stay in the prefab we were disturbed by a mighty hammering on the door. Mr L stood on the doorstep flanked on either side by two of the Polish lodgers. He demanded that I get into the car and return to Salisbury with him immediately. My brothers, hearing raised voices, came to the door and standing one on either side of me said, 'Joan stays here'.

It was music to my ears … wonderful. At last I felt that someone was fighting my corner. Mr L left and I foolishly thought that that would be the last of the L's in my life. (I still haven't worked out how he knew where I was, or how he knew my Mother's address.)

Finding a job

I had two immediate problems, firstly, and most pressing, I needed a ration book, for without it I couldn't eat and secondly I needed a job. Jobs in post-war

Gosport were few and far between; there'd been major bomb damage to the Town, and no factories or industrial units existed, even the cinema was an empty shell of a building. The nearest cinemas were in Portsmouth, but if I went to any of those my wages would be spent travelling across the Harbour everyday. My reference from the Odeon was practically worthless so I signed on at the dole office hoping to find work. We had to sign on Mondays and Wednesdays to say we were not working. On Friday morning I was paid one pound, seventeen shillings and sixpence. My Mother had the one pound for my 'keep' and I was left with the rest. The rules for receiving benefit (or dole money as it was called then) were very strict. Each time I signed on the supervisor would look through her files of job vacancies. If I was handed a card for an interview, I had to keep it, or no money would be paid at the end of the week. The card would be returned to the office saying whether or not the applicant was suitable, if the answer was 'no' the interviewer would state the reason and sign the card to verify that the person had actually turned up. Failure to attend interviews meant an immediate withdrawal of benefit.

One Monday I had a message to see the manager, I thought it would be about a job, but it wasn't. The office had received a letter from Mr L in Salisbury to the effect that I was working in Salisbury during the week and drawing the dole fraudulently! It was a shock for me to have to prove my innocence, but thank goodness I was finally believed. I was very upset by this incident and noticed an advert on the office wall for girls to join the WRNS. It seemed a good idea, so I filled in the application form, sent it off and waited. A few weeks later I received a railway ticket in the post and an appointment in Southampton. I was informed that it would include a medical and aptitude tests to decide which branch I would be most suited for if all went according to plan. All did go according to plan and I was told that as soon as there was a vacancy I would be notified. The branch I chose was S.B.A. (Sick Berth Attendant). At last I would be nursing.

The worst part now was waiting and trying to manage some sort of social life on seven shillings and sixpence a week. I soon worked it out, after all I could now go out when I pleased, so if I went to the Saturday dance held at Lee-on-the-Solent's Tower Ballroom, with a bit of luck I'd have enough dates to take me out for the week! It cost 9d. on the bus to get to Lee and 2/6d. to get in, the bus back to Gosport was provided free. Luckily it was before the days of women's lib; it was still not considered the correct etiquette for females to pay their own way. The Ballroom was shaped like a threepenny bit (a small copper version of today's fifty pence) and there was a bar upstairs. It was still unusual for women to drink (well, in the circles I mixed in it was frowned upon) and for a female to go into a public house without a male escort was a definite 'no-

Social life

no'. There were always more males than females, thanks to all the Navy bases in the Gosport area, so dance partners were never a problem and I still loved to dance. These were the days of the 'Quickstep', 'Waltz' and my particular favourite 'The Foxtrot', I can still hear the dreamy strains of 'Autumn Leaves' in my head, it was a perfect melody for the 'Foxtrot'. I missed out on the craze of 'Jitterbug', which was just as well for I never did get the hang of it! If the dance floor was not as full as it should be, and the males were busy talking instead of dancing, the compère would announce a 'Paul Jones' hoping to encourage everyone onto the dance floor. The males would form an outer circle and walk around clock-wise, while the females formed an inner circle and walked around anti-clockwise, when the music stopped whoever you were facing was your partner for the next dance. It helped the shyer youngsters to meet someone and strike up a conversation, breaking the ice so to speak and hopefully lead to another dance. I think I should mention that I'm not the terrible flirt I appear. I thought of males as friends, with such feelings of low esteem I couldn't possibly think anything else. I admit I found young men much easier to talk to than girls and during my school days I intentionally avoided the complications of having a female best friend.

As I mentioned earlier that females didn't drink and apart from home-made raisin wine at Christmas I wasn't brought up in an environment surrounded by alcohol, my one night of imbibing left me feeling so ill that I had no desire to repeat the experience. One evening at the Lee-on-Solent dance my partner asked me if I would go to the bar with him and have a drink to celebrate his birthday. I said 'Okay' and went upstairs to the bar where he bought me, as it was a special occasion, a Benedictine. I took a large mouthful and wondered what had happened to my voice … I could only gasp in a hoarse whisper as the liquid slowly burnt it's way through my digestive system. He said he was surprised to see me take such a large gulp as it was a liqueur and should be sipped. I haven't tasted a Benedictine since! It's a hard lesson when you're young and trying to act sophisticated.

I remember well the generosity of my elder brother David. He knew I wanted to go to the New Year's Eve dance, but my clothes were still in Salisbury. He took me to the nearest dress shop and paid three pounds and ten shillings for a grey satin dress with a black velvet bodice, the money he paid was more than a week's wages to him. I've never forgotten his kindness and I love him for it.

The NSPCC and Mrs L

The most pressing problem at the moment, apart from finding a job, was having so few clothes to wear. Mother decided we would go to Salisbury with an empty suitcase and try and retrieve some of my belongings. Our first port of call was to see Mr Braggar to ask how I stood legally. He replied, 'I hope Mrs L refuses to let you into the house, for this would give me the opportunity to take her to court; I have a thick file concerning her treatment of you two girls, but I've never had enough evidence to take her to court. I have complaints from neighbours about her mental cruelty to you girls, but it's something that's very hard to prove. However, if she refuses to give you your possessions, I have a case and can introduce my files against her in court.'

I thought it an ideal opportunity to ask him why he'd allowed the L's to adopt us in the first place. His reply: 'As far as I was concerned I was asked to find suitable parents for two girls, a married couple that would be willing to adopt both sisters and keep them together. The girls were not babies, but aged eight and ten, which made it more difficult to find someone who would be prepared to take on the responsibility. On the face of it the L's seemed a respectable couple with a good home, a reasonable income and a car, they were also prepared to adopt both girls.' That's all right then … he was doing us a favour!

Mother and I boarded the bus from the city centre which stopped at the bottom of that hated road which I'd hoped I would never have to walk up again. I was dragging my heels as we walked up the hill and through the gate. I knocked on the front door and Mrs L opened it. I was half expecting her to drag me in, lock the door and all my efforts of escape would have been to no avail. My Mother explained why we had come and she let us in saying: 'Of course you must have your clothes'

Retrieving my clothes

Butter wouldn't melt! While my Mother and Mrs L drank cups of tea in the sitting-room like two old friends at a reunion, I went upstairs and packed my belongings. I was feeling very nervous, my pulse was beating at least double the normal rate, half expecting that awful woman to come up behind me and inflict pain on some part of my body. I couldn't believe it would be this simple, but it was, nothing untoward was said or done. Maybe it was because my Mother was with me, I don't know and I was too scared to say anything. I declined the offer of a cup of tea, I just wanted to get out of the house and breathe in fresh air, so we left as quickly as we could. Once again Mrs L had come up smelling of roses!

I finally received my Naval call-up papers and a rail warrant to Burghfield, near Reading to enlist in the WRNS. I'd begin with four weeks basic training at Burghfield to see if I was suitable. 'Murphy's Law', two weeks before I was due to leave Gosport I was offered a job issuing new Ration Books. I naturally jumped at the chance as it meant I would have some money to take with me and I could clear the debt to my Mother for my green coat. It was a 'doddle' of a job, we sat at large make-shift tables in an old church hall; the public would present us with their old ration books, show us proof of identity and we'd do a bit of rubber stamping and pass on to the next applicant. As I would be wearing uniform from now on I gave my dresses and skirts to my friend. A new beginning all round, I left for the railway station full of hope and optimism.

The WRNS

I don't want to dwell too much on my life in the Navy. It's no different to thousands of other females who have served in the WRNS, started their basic training at Burghfield, learnt to walk like a 'fellah', drunk Shandies in the village pub, where they cost sixpence for a half-pint. (It's becoming increasingly

Chatham RN Hospital

obvious as I write about this era how useful a coin was the humble 'Tanner'). Each new intake thought they were the first group to try and squash down the sides of their hats to give the impression they'd been in the Navy for years. After four weeks of cleaning, learning Naval history and customs, marching and becoming used to drinking from a tin mug the girls who remained were kitted out in uniform. The first day in uniform we were given a pass to the 'Big Smoke' (so called I believe because of the continuous smog that would hang over the Capital before clean fuel was introduced, when it then became illegal to use anything other than smokeless fuel). We tried to avoid the Cenotaph as we felt a bit self-conscious having to salute it as we passed by. For the same reason we couldn't relax in case we passed an officer and forgot to salute, so much to think about now we were members of the Nation's Senior Service and so afraid we would let everyone down. I found refuge in the Nuffield Centre where I learnt how to be alone among a crowd as everyone was in a uniform of some kind, it reminded me of a shoal of fish — all movement and no recognition! Finally, at Burghfield we were to be told where our first posting (or draft) was going to be.

The girls who'd opted for the Medical Branch were to spend the next six months training to be a nurse at Chatham R.N Hospital. When we arrived at the cabin (dormitory) which was to be home for thirty girls there was a 'welcoming party' lined up along the path. These girls were further on in their training by a few weeks which automatically made them senior (actually you were automatically senior if you'd only arrived one day before). The first words I heard were 'Nothing to worry about with this lot, no competition here'.

Strange the things that stick in the mind! We each had an iron bunk bed and a metal locker on our own piece of 'floor-space', but after a wardrobe bed on the landing it seemed more than adequate to me. Most of the time was spent in the classroom learning basic Anatomy and Physiology, or with the 'Schoolie' to take our H.E.T. (Higher Education Test) There was a mixture of males and females in our class but strange as it may seem, girls were not allowed to learn about Venereal Diseases and the boys were excluded from Gynaecology.

After four months in the classroom we were let loose on the wards; to say we were green and inexperienced was being generous. My first spell of 'on-hands' duty consisted of going round the ward of thirty or so patients doing their 'pressure areas'. I would rub soap onto their buttocks followed by white spirit, this was the prescribed preventative treatment against bed-sores. I didn't know the faces of any of the men, but by the end of the week I knew all their backsides! I would progress round the ward mentally reciting, 'fat one,' 'spotty one,' 'hairy one' etc.etc. as I moved from patient to patient. They groaned when they saw me coming and called me 'the nurse with the ice-cold hands'. I think the relief was mutual when I moved on to a more responsible job. A patient had both eyes bandaged and I was told to give him a shave with a cut-throat razor. He said 'I'm very nervous, have you used a cut-throat razor before?' 'Thousands of times' I lied as I proceeded to give him a shave.

It must have been to his satisfaction as he requested I shave him each day until his bandages were removed. There were a lot of Army as well as Naval patients in the hospital at this time, they were suffering from various injuries incurred as they helped in the rescue work during the 1952 East Coast floods. The servicemen were being admitted in droves, mainly with hernias, caused by lifting people and animals from the flooded areas. The storms were a terrible tragedy both to people and livestock, but at least the sea-defences were reinforced soon afterwards to prevent a repeat disaster.

One day I was asked to report to the Third Officer, I couldn't think of anything I'd done wrong, but even so I was feeling a little apprehensive as I stood outside her office door. I was taken aback by what she had to say. The Admiralty had forwarded a letter from Mr L saying he wanted me sent home immediately as I'd joined the WRNS. without his parental permission, failing that, would they forward my address to him so that he could contact me. I question now how he knew I'd joined the Navy, but at that time I felt panic stricken with fear at the thought of being sent back to Salisbury. The Officer explained that I didn't need permission at eighteen years of age and my address would only be forwarded with my consent. It was not given. They replied he could write to The Admiralty in London and his letters would subsequently be forwarded on to me, but no address would be forthcoming. He didn't write again.

Something that seemed strange whilst I was at Chatham was the method by which we were paid. We earned the princely sum of £4 6d. per fortnight, out of which I'd allotted my Mother £1. The Navy only paid us with paper money and no coinage, so we had to wait twenty weeks for the sixpences to add up to ten shillings. I was not in the Navy for the money! A strange sight was when we were told that gas-masks were to be worn on pay-parade. This caused a spectator sport for the patients, they'd lean out of the ward windows, and shout the names of the nurses, trying to identify which nurse was which.

Navy pay

I seemed to spend more time than the other girls at the Dentist. One morning, after two extractions, I was feeling a bit under the weather from the anaesthetic, so instead of returning to the classroom as was expected, I returned to the cabin and lay down on my bunk (a top bunk) and promptly fell asleep. I awoke to the sound of a booming voice saying: 'What's this child doing here?'

I opened my eyes to see that I was surrounded by 'Top Brass' (Officers). It slowly dawned on me that it was 'Admiral's rounds' that day when everything had to be polished, dusted and in its right place, or as you would say 'Ship-Shape and Bristol-Fashion'. Well, I thought, not much I can do at this precise moment in time, I was on my bunk when I was supposed to be in class and my pillow was wet and sticky with blood from my dental treatment. I could hardly

A kind Admiral

jump up, stand to attention and salute pretending nothing was untoward! The Admiral was very kind, he turned to the Chief Wren and said,

'I want you to lightly boil an egg, cut the crusts off some bread and butter, put it on a tray with a cup of tea and bring it here'. He bent forward and said, 'I hope you'll soon be feeling better'.

He then left with his entourage of 'gold-braid'. None of the others believed me when I told them what had happened until the Chief Wren confirmed my story.

We had an examination at the end of our training and if we passed we'd know where we would be stationed on our next posting. When the results were announced I had passed all but one subject – Hygiene. I couldn't believe it. The question only asked me to write about the house-fly, which, with my years of knowledge and experience, I thought a stupid question at the time and wrote about half a page stating the obvious, ' that it was an insect with questionable habits so keep food covered.' This was, after all, a time when most homes hung fly-papers dripping with arsenic over their dining-tables and in their kitchens, only to be renewed when they were covered in dead insects. When I explained this to the P.O. (Petty Officer) he said: 'Don't repeat what you've just said during your oral test with the Commander, he has written umpteen volumes on the ways and habits of the house-fly! it's his pet subject.'

I was a very subdued young lady when I entered the Commander's office, I glanced at all the leather-bound volumes on his bookshelves and knew I'd made an enormous mistake. I was determined not to be so cocksure when he questioned me (I was so humble I could easily have passed an audition for Uriah Heap) … I passed.

A kind Chief Wren Cook

There were a couple of other incidences that show the human side of a large organisation. We were very lucky with our Chief Wren Cook. After a particularly long day on the wards but still being on 'watch' (duty) she would cook us little treats, e.g. breadpudding or a cauliflower cheese. She was like a mother-hen and really spoilt us. Another time the Third Officer took a phone call from a lad I knew in Gosport. He'd managed to get tickets to the London Palladium and said he would meet me at London Bridge Station at six that evening. There was however a small snag, I had no money to get to London. The Third Officer lent me ten shillings, gave me a late pass and said 'enjoy yourself' … I did. The top of the bill was Winnie Attwell. During the first half of the show she played Grieg's piano concerto and in the second half she played Ragtime on what she called ' her other piano'. I wish I could remember the rest of the acts. There was a group of singers from America and various comedians, dancers and acrobats. Sorry folks your names are not in my memory banks, but I think one group was called 'The Deep River Boys'.

In 1952 the big film of the year was *High Noon* and the Third Officer bought a copy of the title song. She would play it over and over until we all knew the words and would sing, 'Do not forsake me, Oh my darling'. It starred Gary Cooper and Grace Kelly and as time has passed it has become a Western classic.

All the nursing staff had to be tested for TB. First we had the 'Mantoux' test and if no reaction appeared we would have to have the new vaccine, B.C.G. (Bacillus of Calmette and Guerin) Unlike the vaccination for smallpox, which left only a mild reaction, this was PAINFUL! After the jab we would wear a red armband for anything up to three weeks to warn people not to bump our arm. One poor lad had such a vicious reaction it looked as if his arm was being eaten away. During my 'red-armband' days I went to the local 'flea-pit' cinema to see the new blockbuster film, *Gone With The Wind*, hoping it would take my mind off the continuous throb- throb- throbbing in my arm. I thought the film was good, but I was disappointed with the abrupt ending. When I mentioned this to one of the girls in the cabin she burst out laughing – I'd left the cinema during the interval! Due to the unusual length of the film the manager had decided to have an interval half way through. Fancy missing Clarke Gable's 'Frankly, my dear, I don't give a damn'!

We had a lot of fun at the Chatham NAAFI Club. It was sixpence (that magic little coin again!) admission charge and although all three services were stationed in and around Chatham, the sailors were very protective towards the WRNS. If a soldier stepped out of line by being too pushy, there was always someone from the hospital to help us out. They also made sure we didn't walk back to the hospital across the Chatham Lines on our own. Mind you, if you were to ask a matelot what he thinks of WRNS he'll say: 'They're rubbish, the Service should never have allowed women into the Navy'. It didn't stop a great number of WRNS becoming Naval wives though!

Chatham NAAFI club

It was at the NAAFI club that I had my first experience of television viewing. The small TV room was jam-packed with service men and women and all the seats were taken, I barely managed to squeeze through the door and find just enough room to stand with my back pressed against the wall. The room was filled with cigarette smoke, making it even more difficult to see the picture on the small screen, but I had to make a hasty retreat when I doubled up with a fit of the giggles. The trouble began when Anne Shelton appeared on the screen and started to sing; she was not a slim lady and her dress was very low cut at the front revealing her sizeable bust. Something was wrong with the line-hold and there was this poor lady, unaware of the picture quality, wobbling up and down like a jelly on a plate! Hilarious! I wasn't in a hurry to own a television set.

Television

One weekend, a male nurse working on the same ward as myself asked if I'd like to go to his home for the weekend instead of staying on board, I said 'Yes' and on Friday evening we travelled to London. His mother was a widow whose husband had been killed during the war and he had two younger sisters. During dinner, the mother made statements in my direction such as, 'My son is too young to marry' and 'It'll be years before he wants to settle down'. I don't know what he'd told her about his guest but I spoke the truth when I said: 'I agree, he's much too young for commitments'.

Record players

The mother went to bed early leaving us with a record player and a pile of records. Record players only played one side of the disc at a time and then they had to be manually turned over. Each time the music stopped there was a loud banging on the floor-boards from upstairs and a new record was hastily put onto the turn-table. If she'd taken the trouble to come down stairs she would have seen her precious boy sitting on the floor by the pile of records, while I was quite comfortably curled up on the settee reading a book. I found the situation hilarious as I had absolutely no designs on her darling boy. Luckily I had a new novel by Richard Gordon called *Doctor in the House*; it struck the right chord with someone who was training to be a nurse and I chuckled my way through to the end. On Sunday afternoon we returned to the hospital.

Engagement

I became engaged to a patient while I was at Chatham. He also came from London and his ambition was to become a professional ball-room dancer. He was literally tall, dark and handsome. He asked the manager of the NAAFI club if we could use the ballroom to practise our steps during closing hours. He agreed and even allowed us to borrow records and use the record player. Sunday mornings we had the ballroom to ourselves. I could dance, but not to his high standard, however, once on the dance-floor and with him leading, I found my feet doing steps I didn't know I was capable of mastering, I think it also helped my confidence that there was no-one else around whilst we were practising. We became well known for our expertise when we danced and on occasions drew quite an audience. It was a very happy period in my life. He took me to meet his parents in London and although his father was very friendly towards me, his step-mother seemed more interested in getting him married off as soon as possible. I'll mention the reason for our break up later on, but for the moment my life seemed to be taking on some kind of direction.

I did have some problems with the communal living arrangements. I couldn't understand the reason why some of the girls shared each others' bunk-beds. I'd never heard of lesbians or homosexuals, they were words I'd never come across in my eighteen years of life. I was also shocked by a couple of WRNS who would go to Maidstone at weekends and proudly count their money when they returned on Sunday evening; money they'd earned from American soldiers! I wasn't a prude, but this seemed unacceptable behaviour to me. Needless to say I was pretty miserable, so one weekend I went home to tell my Mother what was going on and said, 'I'm unhappy and don't like what's going on, I don't want to go back'. She replied, 'It's life, you'll have to put up with it'.

I think the occasional visits at weekends were welcome, we were given food-coupons for our two days away from the hospital and this was always most welcome. Sometimes my brothers would also be home on weekend leave, which was good from my point of view as I felt we had a lot of 'catching up' to do. I remember one weekend I took four friends home with me and as my brothers were also home, sleeping arrangements in a two-bedroom prefab. caused a problem. My Mother went to bed early, suffering with one of her migraines, but the five girls and my two brothers all slept on mattresses on the floor in the other bedroom. It was quite a squash, but we all managed without any embarrassment (everyone wore pyjamas in those days).

There was a buzz of excitement, mixed with slight feelings of trepidation, when we were told we were going to watch a surgeon perform an operation. If we felt ill, we were to leave the theatre immediately, and if we fainted we would be left where we fell to come round in our own time. The boys were naturally full of bravado and teasing the girls about blood and gore (as boys do). We were to watch the removal of half a lung damaged by TB. Once in the theatre I thought the part of the body to be cut resembled a joint of pork, it had already been given a painting of iodine and only the area to be cut was uncovered. I thought, this is fine. It fascinated me as the surgeon made his incision, I could see the patient's heart beating beneath the ribs before they were cut to enable the surgeon to get to the lung. At the end of the operation only the female students were left in the theatre, the boys had all left, one by one!

RNH Haslar

When the examinations were over we looked forward to our next draft. I was hoping to go to Scotland or Ireland, but the Scots girls were sent to Ireland or Cornwall, and the Cornish or Devon girls were sent to Scotland. There was one draft to Gosport and it was mine. I felt terribly disappointed, so much for the saying 'join the Navy and see the world'. HUH! My posting was to RNH Haslar. Accommodation at the hospital was for the VADs (Voluntary Aid Detachment) and the WRNS were billeted in HMS Collingwood, a Naval establishment half way between Gosport and Fareham. We had a wooden hut which some wag informed us was the old mortuary, at the back of the ship (all Naval shore bases are called ships) and it was a very strange routine we embarked upon. The hours on the wards were, (day one) 8a.m. to 8p.m., (day two) 8a.m..to 6p.m., (day three) 8a.m. to 1p.m., then it was back to (day one). Night duty lasted for four weeks, or to be exact twenty-eight nights, 8p.m. to 8a.m. without a break, followed by four days off. Good job I was used to long hours! A Naval van would pick us up from Collingwood and drive us to Haslar in time for an 8a.m. start on the wards, then we would be driven back at the end of our 'watch' (duty) to Collingwood. Food was a bit of a lottery. Breakfast was fine, we were there for the first serving, but when we finished at 1p.m. we arrived half an hour later to find dinners on a hotplate that had been nicely drying out since noon! Supper was served from 6p.m., so when we arrived back for food at 8.30p.m. it was so dried up as to be almost inedible. By then, though, we were so tired that all we wanted to do was fall into bed. Because of the catering arrangements we preferred the longer shifts; we could then eat in the VADs' mess at lunch-time. Their standard of living was so much superior to ours, the difference was incredible. Tables were laid with white linen tablecloths and sets of gleaming cutlery, there were even vases of flowers in the centre of each table and waitresses to serve the food The menus were varied and the food well cooked, it was a delight. I found this a wee bit confusing, VAD courses were identical to ours, but they were treated as if they were something special, even the Ward Sisters and Doctors treated them with more respect than the Naval nurses.

I'm the first to admit that nursing and I were not wholly compatible. I was fine on the medical wards but pretty squeamish on the surgical wards, I couldn't detach myself from their pain. The other problem I had was after a patient had died, the grieving relatives were a forgotten entity, whereas I thought the living relatives needed more care than the dead body! There was an old-fashioned profession called an 'Almoner' and I think that would have been a more suitable path for me to take. Today, I suppose, they'd be called Social Workers.

One morning a patient was being discharged and he asked if I'd meet him in Portsmouth at half-past three that afternoon and see a film before he caught his train home for sick-leave. As my duty finished at one o'clock that day I said, 'Yes'. I'd have time to return to Collingwood and change into a clean shirt before catching the ferry from Gosport to Portsmouth. As I went through the

HM Queen Elizabeth II

ship's gates I was told that all leave had been cancelled as the Queen would be passing by the ship in the afternoon and we were detailed to line the sides of the road and cheer as she drove by. We lined up and waited and waited, however, when the car did finally arrive we had a clear view of our new Queen as she passed by in an open topped car. (My memory holds the strange fact of how beautifully matched were her lipstick and coat!). I didn't arrive in Portsmouth until 5p.m., so if a certain Chief wondered why the nurse stood him up … that's why!

Living in my home-town gave me plenty of opportunity to visit home and of course my Grandmother Russell, whose health was beginning to give cause

Portsmouth NAAFI club

for alarm. I also spent most of my leisure time at the Portsmouth NAAFI club, mainly because it was cheap (still the magic entry fee of sixpence) but also because it was more of a social club than anything else in the area, there was the bar and dancing every night except Sunday … everything that was fun was banned on Sundays. The club had a record booth where we could sit and listen to the latest music from America, as well as popular songs from this country. This was the age of 'big bands' and ballads performed by artists such as Denis Lotis, Nat King Cole, Bing Crosby, Dickie Valentine, Perry Como and my still favourite, Frankie Laine. There was news of some upstart in America who thought he could croon better than Bing … his name was Frank Sinatra. The music of Tommy Dorsey, Stan Kenton, Joe Loss, Ted Heath, Oscar Rabin and Tito Burns. The latter had a radio programme that he introduced by saying: 'Hold your seats while Tito Bu-u-u-u-rns'.

Female vocalists in vogue were Eve Boswell, Alma Cogan, Doris Day, Ella Fitzgerald, Jo Stafford, Rose Murphy and Joan Regan, all their songs had words

Popular songs

which were easy to learn and lyrics we could sing along with. After saying that I'd better mention 'Mareseatoats, doeseatoats and little lambs eativy' so I suppose we did have our share of silly songs. The dance music scene was dominated by the strict tempo music of Victor Sylvester, he really cornered the market with his unique sound of dance music. It was a time when errand-boys could still whistle to the tune of popular songs and ballads had words to tear at the heart strings.

I now knew the name of a drink I enjoyed … 'Tom Collins'. I didn't like the taste of beer and the only other drink I knew the name of was 'Port and Lemon', but that conjured up a memory of being 'leg-less' one Christmas. One of the WRENS would bet the sailors that she could drink a pint of beer in one go; she made quite a bit of money at half-a-crown a time. Not very lady-like I thought. Although I was still engaged I didn't see my fiancé very often, he was still serving at Chatham, but letters were frequent and occasionally he would stay the weekend at my Mother's prefab. We were allowed one weekend pass a month, but first it had to be signed by your parent or guardian to verify that you were staying at the address on the pass. The same rule applied when females wanted to spend a weekend at the NAAFI club in Chatham. The rules at the club were very strict and no males could go anywhere near the women's quarters, it was like having your own guard dog. There were rooms for married couples, but they had to show their marriage licence at the time the room was booked. My fiancé and I would eat breakfast together and then practise dancing in the ballroom until lunchtime. After lunch, more dance practice untill the club opened in the evening. He did tell me that his future plans didn't include children, as they would curtail his dancing ambitions.

I was now enjoying life as people do who don't stop to think, a prerogative only enjoyed by the young! I was either working, dancing, writing letters, feeling hungry or visiting my Grandmother. After one of my longer shifts I picked up two letters from my mail rack, both were postmarked Chatham and both of them were in NAAFI envelopes. I recognised the writing on one, but not the other, then I remembered I had been dancing a couple of times with a sailor who was going to Chatham on a course. I was not prepared for what I read. Two matelots writing to their girlfriend in Gosport, sitting opposite each other in the NAAFI club writing-room, started up a conversation, exchanged pictures of their beloved and … SNAP same girl! … what a long-shot. No more trips to Chatham. Strangely enough I wasn't too upset, I think it was just another relationship I'd drifted into without much thought, still not taking declarations of love seriously.

No longer engaged

In January 1953 there was a very bad outbreak of 'flu (influenza) whilst I was stationed at HMS Collingwood. The sickbay was turned into a mini hospital ward to cope with the number of sailors falling sick. The Medical Branch's first priority was to vaccinate as many of the men as possible to prevent the flu spreading further, I was one of the nurses taken off the wards to help. I had never given an injection, and to say I was petrified would be an understatement. It's quite incredible how little training we had before being thrown in at the 'deep end' so to speak One male nurse who sensed my uneasiness, sug-

'Flu

gested I should practise on an orange, as it had a tough outer layer and a soft centre, thus resembling skin. I hadn't practised and I dreaded the job. I stood by the medical trolley, needles at the ready, facing the long queue with an air of pseudo nonchalance, knowing that if anyone spoke to me I would be incapable of uttering anything louder than a 'squeak' A junior doctor came up to me and said, 'I'll do the necessary, nurse, you just keep filling the syringes'.

I could have hugged him but I didn't know the Naval punishment rules on familiarity with Officers from lower ranks, … phew, what a relief!

The next twenty-eight nights were spent on duty in the sick bay. It was a reasonably easy duty as the patients mainly slept, but the food provided for the nurses was certainly not supplied with any thought to diet or nutrition. For all the twenty-eight nights the chef left us bacon, egg, tomatoes and bread in the galley for our meal; occasionally it would be varied with a couple of sausages instead of bacon. This is not a recommended diet. No daylight and eating only fried food makes the skin very dry. When we finished our duty at eight o'clock in the morning we were just in time for a fried breakfast! I found the worst time to stay awake on 'nights' was around four in the morning; the desire to sleep was overwhelming, the eyelids would become leaden, it was a fight to keep awake. We would play draughts to keep our brains alert until six o'clock when we'd wake the patients with a cup of tea and the next day's routine would begin. If I had been left to my own devices I could easily have slept for twelve hours, but made do with eight. These twenty eight days of non-stop duty did have one advantage … my pay lasted longer and I could buy some clothes with the money I'd saved. I still managed to keep up with the gossip however, all the 'on-off' romances and who was dating who (what else is of interest to a group of young females living so close to each other?).

I was told by one of the girls that she had become engaged to one of the male nurses at Haslar, her news surprised me a little as I'd heard his name mentioned by several of the other girls who'd also been dated by him. I thought he was just working his way through all the nurses. When 'nights' had finished I started my four days leave and went to the NAAFI club … where else? I saw the two nurses together at the bar and, as one does, I went over and congratulated them. She gave me a 'drop-dead' look and he stormed out of the bar! His mate told me that it was news to him that he was engaged! The next day in the hospital canteen I was told that a coffee was waiting for me at the table of this so called fiancé. He apologised for the previous evening and asked me if I would I go out with him that night. I declined his kind offer, I thought I must now be the last nurse on his list. I was dancing that evening at the NAAFI club when the male nurse arrived, walked up to me on the dance floor and asked me for my coat tag. He fetched my coat and we left, but he only accompanied me as far as the bus stop! It was the first time I'd arrived back at the ship early and I was not amused! This was repeated several times and I was quite mystified by his behaviour, sort of him Svengali and me Trilby (except that I lacked any talent as regards singing). He said he wanted me to give him any spare wool left over by the patients from their rug-making occupational therapy. He was making a wool rug to his own design and didn't see the need of the expense of buying wool when there were all these spare 'thrums' going begging on the ward. I was working on the medical ward at the time and most of the patients were diagnosed as suffering from ulcers. Their treatment entailed long bed-rest, Aludrox, stopping smoking and an awful bland diet of steamed fish and milk puddings. The nurse was quite correct though about the wool and the patients were only too happy to give me their left overs, so each day I would meet the nurse in the canteen and hand over my meagre gleanings.

The pattern of our daily meetings ended abruptly when I started four weeks' night duty, this time on the female ward in the hospital. When I worked 'nights' I could only sleep during the day, I had no energy left for socialising. How these people who work at night manage with half a day's sleep is a mystery to me, I had a job to wake up after six hours' sleep and be back on duty in time. The food was a great improvement as well because we could have dinner in the VAD hall before going on duty and there was plenty of bread in the galley at night which we toasted, I think my main food intake during this four week period was toast! Surprise, surprise, this nurse would come into the ward galley around midnight and ask for a cup of tea or some toast. He even asked me one night if I would syringe his ears. He must have regretted that as I nearly drowned him in the process ... well, it was the first time I'd done 'ears' and things are very different in practice from what they are in theory aren't they? I was beginning to liken him to a flea that I couldn't shake off!

Another problem at this time was Grandmother Russell. Although it's a bit harsh to say she was a problem, what I really mean is that her health was giving rise for concern and she needed someone with her all the time.

An arrangement was made that as Mother worked during the day, she would spend the night at Gran's, and as I worked at night I would stay with her during the day.

She'd had a hard life and was a deeply religious lady. After she was widowed she would stand at the bottom of Pneumonia Bridge (which crossed from Gosport to Haslar) stopping the sailors going ashore to the numerous pubs in Gosport and encouraging them to go to the Bethel Mission for Sailors instead of drinking their hard earned wages. Her living accommodation was very sparse and she had no luxuries or mod cons in her two-up two-down house. The five houses in the row shared two taps and two lavatories in the cobbled yard outside their front doors. There was a black range which she used for both cooking and heating. There was no electricity and gas mantles provided her with light in the winter evenings, the only picture on the wall was a sepia print of Jesus holding a lantern. During the war an unexploded bomb put a large hole in her bedroom ceiling, from then on she slept downstairs. Outside her front window there was a profusion of golden nasturtiums covering her Anderson shelter. Her rent was 5/- a week from her meagre State Pension of 10/-. Throughout her hard life she made the most colourful patchwork bedspreads; I can see her now, stitching brightly patterned scraps of material onto diamond-shaped pieces of newspaper. The only piece of jewellery I can ever remember her wearing was a mother-of-pearl brooch which in reality was the end of a cotton reel, I thought it looked like a shiney doily, and her wedding ring. It was during this time that I heard the story of 'I'm looking forward to dying and meeting my sailor lover again'.

The story she confided in me said: 'I fell in love with a handsome sailor, but as he was not my social equal my Father paid the sailor to return to the sea. I never saw or heard from him again. The decorators were working for my parents at the time and in a fit of youthful pique I ran away and married the decorator'.

She was immediately disowned by her family. I have to remember that this happened during Victorian times when fathers were very strict about their social standing and dictated who their daughters could or could not marry. My Grandfather was a jeweller and successful property owner and such was the strength of the class system in the nineteenth century that a father's word was law. She had a very hard life and suffered eight miscarriages. Her husband (who died before I was born) was a heavy drinker and when he returned drunk from the pub he would 'slap her around a bit' (this is a quote by her son) and the inevitable miscarriage would result. She always dressed smartly and would wear white insets in the top of her dresses, she would plait her white hair before winding it round in a circle to be kept in place with hair-pins to form a neat and tidy' bun' at the nape of her neck, I doubt she ever knew the luxury of sitting in a hair salon and having her hair dressed professionally. How she managed to come to terms with her 'lot' I'll never know, but she showed an inner strength which I could only admire. Three of her children survived, but even then she lost her youngest son, Ernie, during the Second World War. It was only her strong belief in God that sustained her. She was a very proud lady and I loved her dearly.

One day while I was looking after my Grandmother, my hair in 'dinkey' curlers under a turban, there was a knock on the back door. I was black-leading the range at the time and I'd managed to get black smudges on my face and half way up my arms, I was wearing an old overall and felt that it's not really the way a girl likes to be caught. I opened the door and it was my 'Svengali'. He'd found out from my Mother where I was staying during the day and thought he would call to see me. He told me he loved me. Now ... I was lacking sleep, looked awful with black smudges on my face and arms ... quite a comical sight for an onlooker, I suppose. My immediate reaction was 'What a send-up! ' but I gave him ten out of ten for perseverance. His name was Larry and he continued to pop up unexpectedly during the day at Grandmother's or in the ward galley at night. I was past caring what I looked like, I wasn't trying

Larry perseveres

to impress him so I didn't see the need to make an effort and luckily he didn't ask for repeat treatment for his ears!

Night duty over, I was looking forward to my four days' leave. The tenants of the prefabs had all been offered first refusal on the new houses being built by the council. This was not unexpected as the prefabs were only given a life-span of ten years, they were temporary accommodation until the post-war building programme was up and running. Mother accepted a new house and this is where I would stay for my four days' leave and try catching up on some much needed sleep. The situation at my Grandmother's could not go on this way either, my Mother was worn out and I was about to return to day duty on the wards, the obvious solution was for her to leave her home and occupy the spare room at Mother's. During the day a home-help would come and sit with Gran, do some cleaning or shopping, but mainly be with her and ease the strain on Mother.

One afternoon I was relaxing and chatting to my younger brother, who was on leave at the time and listening to records. My brothers liked Phil Harris's song about the *Gambler* and 'Woodman, woodman spare that tree, Chop not a single bough'. Les Paul and Mary Ford, Jo Stafford and Mantovani with his singing violins were Mother's favourites. Larry was talking about gambling on the horses, how sometimes you win and sometimes you lose. I was half con-centrating, enjoying the relaxed atmosphere and not really listening to what was being said, giving an occasional 'Yes' here and there. He suddenly jumped up from the sofa, went over to my brother and said: 'Your sister has just agreed to be my wife'.

Larry wins

No-one was more surprised than me! Mother came home from work and was told the news. She said: 'Good, you're just right for Joan as she needs someone who won't let her have her own way'. (I'm still trying to work that one out, as getting my own way is a luxury that seemed to have eluded me up to now.) Everyone seemed to be happy for me, maybe I'd missed something in all the excitement, but no matter how many times I went over the afternoon's conversations in my mind I couldn't for the life of me remember something as important as a marriage proposal or an acceptance.

Events over the next few weeks spiralled completely out of hand. Things concerning my future were being decided between third parties, I seemed to have lost all control of my own destiny. I would work on the wards, eat and sleep, but others were making the arrangements and telling me what progress was being made. The significant date was to be 13 June, am I superstitious? I don't know, I didn't have the time or the energy to think about it. Mother went to see the vicar and booked the church for eleven a.m., she did this as we were both working long shifts and didn't have much spare time. I said I would get married in a suit, but Mother said I would always regret it if I didn't wear 'white'. I explained that my finances were zero but it didn't seem to register as a valid reason for not being a traditional bride with all the trimmings. Nobody

Wedding preparations

was listening to me, I had somehow become invisible. To prove her point Mother took me to a shop called 'Nora's' in Portsmouth where they hired out wedding dresses, the veil and even the shoes, (may I suggest flat heels as you're so tall ... ugh!). Everything loaned at a price really, except the bouquet and a bridegroom! ... perhaps I could hire a pretend vicar. I was being swept, or maybe pushed would be a more honest description, along on a tidal wave wondering where it was all going to end. I wasn't excited or joyful and definitely not glowing with happiness. Why didn't someone noticed my reticence? One thing I did insist on though, if we were to spend the rest of our lives together, was that I'd meet his relatives before I committed myself to married life, after all they were to become my in-laws and for all I knew they could be living in a tent in the middle of a field and be the weirdest group of people on this earth! Larry assured me it wasn't necessary as I could meet them after we were man and wife, but on this point I dug in my heels and insisted – no meeting – no wedding. I won the argument, in retrospect it was the first and only argument I ever won!

Lincoln

On the Friday two weeks before the wedding we travelled to Lincoln with our weekend passes. At least I was seeing a different part of the country; I'd travelled as far west as Weymouth with the L's and the furthest north was a trip to Wantage in Berkshire to see the place where 'Girlie' the dog came from, so travelling as far as Lincoln was quite an outing. There was one scary moment in London – I boarded the tube train to take us from Waterloo to Paddington and when the doors closed, I was on the train, my future husband still on the platform with his 'grip' (travelling bag) stuck between the doors and him still holding on to it as the train pulled out of the station! Luckily he managed to free the 'grip'. Fortunately Larry had told me which station we were going to so I had to wait for him to follow on the next train, It felt good to be in 'civvies' (civilian clothes) instead of uniform, at this time we were not allowed to leave the Ship (camp) in 'civvies', uniform had to be worn at all times. During my stay in Chatham I'd bought a grey suit from a shop called 'Wilsons' that allowed the Navy personnel to purchase clothes on 'tick' or 'never-never' (pay as you wear). At times I could understand why it was called 'never-never' as the payments seemed to go on and on. All you had to do was sign an allotment form, agreeing to a certain amount to be deducted from your pay each week; the shops were very keen to sell to servicemen and women as payments were guaranteed. (Another tangent!)

A Lincolnshire home

I was not prepared for my future spouse's home. It was a terrace house with the front door opening straight on to the street, no front garden gate, no garden at the rear, just a cobbled yard. There was no sign of a bathroom or indoor lavatory. I sound like a terrible snob but I truly didn't know that houses like this existed. I learnt that Larry's parents were divorced and his Father was living with his married sister. I had never seen people eat so much in my life, or a woman cook so much as his Aunt. His Father was a butcher and meat was plentiful, it appeared that food rationing had passed them by, but even so the amount of food consumed seemed a bit excessive. Lincolnshire is a county that is renowned for its garden produce and vegetables were in abundance and cheap. Potatoes were one penny a pound, so for one shilling (five new pence) you could buy twelve pounds of potatoes! The whole day revolved around food in my future in-laws' home, even while they were eating, the next meal was being discussed. Breakfast would consist of bacon, eggs, fried bread, tomatoes, mushrooms and kidneys; at midday, a full roast dinner was prepared with vegetables and Yorkshire Pudding, this was followed by a home-made fruit pie or crumble, custard or milk pudding as a dessert. In the early evening they had what they called 'high-tea', this would be either fish or cold meat with salad, bread and margarine (butter was still rationed), home made cakes and pastries; and finally, before retiring at the end of the day, the Aunt would fry-up the left over vegetables from lunch time to be eaten with cold meat from the remainder of the joint! I had nightmarish visions of spending the rest of my life tied to the cooker and kitchen sink, getting fatter and fatter as the years went by ... it was not a pleasant thought.

They were however, very welcoming, though I sensed that they thought southern girls were stuck-up and hopeless at cooking, definitely not what they thought of as 'good-wife' material! That night when I wanted to use the bathroom, I had a bit of a shock when I discovered the lavatory was at the bottom of the yard. It was pouring with rain, the wind was howling (well it was the month of May in England) it was pitch dark and I was only wearing my pyjamas. The Aunt handed me a torch and an old mackintosh, I shone the torch to see where I was going as the Aunt pointed vaguely from the back door towards the end of the yard. The lavatory was a big, square wooden contraption and when I looked for the toilet paper I was even more stunned, there were squares of newspaper tied on a piece of string! My first purchase the following morning was a roll of toilet paper and I made sure I went to the lavatory before turning in for the night!

The Aunt was very gracious and allowed us to sit in the front parlour in the evenings, I think this was a great honour as it had the smell of a room that's seldom used. Saturday morning we walked around Lincoln Market. I was reminded of Salisbury with all the stallholders coming from the surrounding farms to sell their home-grown produce. I couldn't help but be fascinated by the 'pea-stall,' it was surrounded by men holding small saucers and eating peas drenched in vinegar. I did like the sight of each male carrying a bunch of flowers though, a custom a lot of southern men could adopt for their hard-working wives. Saturday afternoon we visited my future mother-in-law, this was grudgingly done but I was curious to see the lady that no one said a kind word about. I was actually quite taken aback, she was very tall and stately, her jet black hair was cut very short and styled with 'Marcel waves' pressed tight to her head. Her home was constructed of wood and the floors were all highly polished with just a few occasional rugs. I was most impressed and couldn't understand how she'd caused so much animosity. The visit was brief and we never saw her again ... to mention her name from then on was strictly 'taboo'.

Saturday evening we went to the local Conservative Club, where I received a further lesson in the great divide between north and south, although to be exact we were only in the Midlands. The ladies were not permitted in the bar, they sat huddled together in a small room off the foyer, and I mean 'small'. There was a coffee table for the ash-trays and drinks and half a dozen chairs standing against the walls. Every so often a spouse would appear with a drink, only to disappear again to the bar and his all male environment. If the male was enjoying himself and the last thing on his mind was his female companion, she could sit for hours staring at an empty glass! I was a stranger in a room full of middle-aged ladies and could only sit there with my fruit juice and cigarettes bored out of my tiny mind, listening to the conversations about children and general tittle-tattle, definitely not my idea of a weekly treat! As my intended had intimated he would leave the Navy in three years' time and we'd live in Lincoln ... I was not a particularly happy girl, continuous cooking and boring Saturday nights out to the club didn't hold much appeal. I would need more than a weekly bunch of flowers to keep me amused!

Lincoln Cathedral   We found time to visit Lincoln Cathedral, which, like Salisbury's Cathedral dominated the City. The difference for me between the two was that Salisbury Cathedral was situated in a valley and appeared stately with it's tall gracious spire, while Lincoln Cathedral appeared square, standing on the top of the hill and looking down on the City. We disagreed over which Cathedral was the superior, but I still think Salisbury wins hands down! The road leading up to the Cathedral was called 'Jews Hill' and to walk up it is only for the very fit or foolhardy. The road was full of old book shops and jewellers that looked as if they'd been selling there since the birth of the town. Cycles were banned, though I can't believe any one would argue with that, you must walk to appreciate the fascinating old shops and architecture, definitely a tourist's 'must-see'. I had my ears pierced in a very dusty back room belonging to a jeweller, and Larry bought me a pair of gold earrings in the shape of a 'Lincoln Imp'. I don't think the hygiene was a hundred percent as my ears were still infected eighteen months later so I gave up wearing earrings for pierced ears. The High Street was dominated by the wonderful aroma of coffee, it permeated the air and we couldn't resist walking towards the tantalising smell, until we finally sat in the restaurant and drank the hot black liquid in the Coffee House. Salisbury couldn't match that!

On Sunday we visited a friend for lunch, we ate the standard Roast Beef and Yorkshire Pudding while listening to 'Family Favourites' on the radio followed by 'The Billy Cotton Band Show'. I think every home in Britain listened to Jean Metcalf and Cliff Michelmore playing requests from soldiers in BFPO (British Forces Post Office) in Germany and messages from home to the troops. Just as people were feeling relaxed and bloated from eating their dinner and listening to the romantic songs from separated loved ones, they were jolted back to the present with Billy Cotton's raucous 'Wakey Wa—-key' coming over the airways.

We said our goodbyes late on Sunday evening. We'd planned to travel through the night on the 'milk-train', hopefully this would give us about fifteen minutes to change into our uniforms and be on the wards for duty at eight o'clock on Monday morning. The train was late, but strangely no-one complained, we seemed to take it in our stride. Perhaps the 'War' had taught us to be more tolerant, I don't really know but we didn't gripe over every little hiccup, we were just so relieved that things were gradually getting back to some semblance of normality. When the train finally arrived it was packed solid with people in various uniforms, Army, Navy and Air Force personnel all returning from a week-end pass and making their way back to camps, airfields and ships. Those lucky enough to have seats were trying to catch up on their sleep, some were even trying to sleep in the corridors using their 'hold-alls' (canvas bags) or cases as pillows. We managed to find a space to stand in the corridor. What a journey! As it was a milk train it stopped and started at every small station on the way … this was pre-Beeching when there were plenty of small stations *en route* to the big cities. The atmosphere though was marvellous, everyone talking and joking and there was a general air of *bon homie*. These were the days when it was perfectly safe for a female to travel alone without worrying whether she would be attacked or worse. When we finally reached London we made a mad dash to Waterloo Station, hoping to grab a seat on the Portsmouth train and perhaps snatch forty-winks before arriving at Portsmouth's Harbour Station. We made another dash to catch the ferry to Gosport, we walked over Pneumonia Bridge and arrived bleary eyed at Haslar Hospital just in time to go on duty. Luckily for me I was on the shorter shift that day.

There was a funny incident I remember in 1953. My Mother would spend every Saturday morning buying her vegetables and fruit in Charlotte Street market in Portsmouth; the majority of traders were upright and honest but there was the occasional 'Del-Boy'! Nylon stockings were still very expensive and hard to come by, but on this particular Saturday a man was selling nylons at five pairs for one pound. Common sense should have prevailed, but nylons and women, plus a bargain, irresistible! We arrived home with our purchases, made the proverbial cup of tea and started to unwrap our precious stockings. First my Mother held up a pair, then I did the same, when we reached the final stocking we were laughing as much from embarrassment at wasting our money as at being duped. We knew we should have 'smelt a rat'. The outcome? … we managed one wearable pair of nylons each, the rest had seams running up the front, up the sides or double seams at the back, they were totally unwearable … it was an expensive lesson.

Charlotte Street market, Portsmouth

The next hurdle was something I was dreading. As I was only nineteen years old I had to have the Ls signed permission to get married, they were still my

Permission required

legal parents, so there was no alternative but to pay them a visit My intended bridegroom wrote a formal letter to the Ls asking for my hand in marriage. I caught the train on the Friday afternoon to Salisbury. Mr L was pleased to see me and said he'd give his permission on one condition ... I was to live with them after I was married! I don't like lying, but this seemed to be one of those circumstances when a black lie was permissible. That evening Mr L took me to see my sister, she and her husband were living in a village near Salisbury. I hadn't seen Joy since the Friday morning she'd left the Ls. Before we drove out into the country we called in at the doctor's; Mr L was suffering with bad chest pains, he was told it was probably an ulcer and was prescribed a bottle of antacid. I was a proper little 'know-all' regarding ulcers. I was working on the gastric ward at the time and was familiar with 'Aludrox', boiled fish and bedrest as a treatment. During the drive to see Joy however, I thought he was trying to kill us both. His driving along the dark, twisting country lanes was erratic to say the least, it was very frightening. We arrived safely though and I had a good chat with my sister. She agreed to be my Matron-of-Honour at the wedding and she'd wear the blue dress I'd worn as a bridesmaid. When we arrived back at the Ls it was arranged for me to sleep with Mrs L (horrible thought) while her husband had a bed made up on the dining-room draw-leaf table. I awoke in the early hours to a groaning sound coming from the kitchen so I went downstairs to investigate. Mr L was holding his chest and said the pain was terrible. He looked very grey and drawn so I knew he was suffering. I made him take some of his 'Aludrox' and waited until he settled back to sleep. Two hours later he was dead. The doctor said he'd probably died of a thrombosis, caused by years of injecting himself with insulin for his diabetes. I think that twenty or thirty years later he would have been diagnosed differently and would probably have lived much longer, but this was still pre-N.H.S. and fantastic improvements in the diagnosis and treatment of heart disease.

Permission granted

I returned to Gosport with the signed marriage consent form and a promise to return to Mrs L after the honeymoon, but now I had to return to Salisbury the following week for the funeral. There was yet another old man staying with the Ls. (I don't know where they found them) and his distress was awful to witness, I think Mr L had befriended him and the thought of his not being there was too much for the poor old soul to bear; as the coffin was being lowered into the grave he tried to jump in with it, he was so distraught. I managed to persuade him to sit with me in the car and when we arrived back at the house I took him up to the small bedroom, made him a cup of sweet tea and let him get into the bed hoping that some sleep would calm him. Mrs L was furious, his bed was on the landing and I'd put him in someone else's bed, I told her he was to stay there for medical reasons and as there was a roomful of mourners she couldn't pursue the argument. He was safe for a while at least. It's said revenge is sweet and through all those years of abuse at the hands of Mrs L I made a promise to myself that one day I would slap her hard across the face. I never thought the opportunity would arise, but it did! After the funeral service, various neighbours and friends were popping in and out to offer their condolences to the 'bereaved' widow. Each time a new face arrived Mrs L went into near hysterics of grief but as soon as they'd left she was eating and talking as if nothing had happened … the performance warranted an Oscar at least! I witnessed this carry on three or four times and decided what to do the next time it happened. Just as if a film director had shouted 'Camera, Lights, Action' her performance began. I walked across the room and slapped her soundly across the face! Her expression was a picture! I explained, that as a nurse I had been taught that the best cure for hysteria was a good sharp slap on the face, she had no answer to that. The feeling I had was the same euphoria as someone winning the lottery … fan-tas-tic!

PART FOUR

1953–70

JUST TEN WEEKS AFTER MEETING LARRY, AND FOUR OF THOSE SPENT ON night duty, we were to be married. My Mother told me he was ideal for me as he wouldn't let me have the upper hand, and I was well trained in doing as I was told. Secretly I kept hoping it would all fizzle out, we were still strangers, he was not very talkative and apart from saying he hoped to return to Lincoln in three years' time I had no idea of his likes or dislikes or even what his aspirations were for the future. I'd had several proposals before and been engaged, but I'd still managed to remain single. In my heart of hearts I didn't quite believe that a wedding would take place and we'd be together for the rest of our lives. Divorce was not a word that immediately sprung to mind in the 1950s and once the ceremony had taken place, that was it. I wasn't in love and I don't think Larry was either, I think his home background made him believe that he needed a home life of his own and he'd selected me as the female of his future house-hold. Maybe I'd be drafted to the Outer Hebrides or some other distant part of the UK, anything that would give me space to think. (Perhaps I was an ostrich in an earlier life.) No draft appeared!

I was discharged from the Navy, as was routine when WRNS were to be married and I now felt like a lemming heading toward the edge of a cliff. The day came and all the plans were in place, my sister and her husband, my friend Ethel who was to be a bridesmaid and my eldest brother David, who'd agreed to give me away, had all arrived. Everyone seemed happy and excited for me. The relatives and future Father-in-law arrived from Lincoln. Mrs L, Aunt May and Uncle Bert were there, but I still couldn't get into the spirit of things. My wedding day coincided with the Queen's Review of the Fleet at Spithead, sadly I would miss the spectacle. The weather was fine, it was one of those June days that were a mixture of sunshine, high cloud and light winds. We'd been allowed to pick roses from a friend's garden to make bouquets for the bridesmaid and Matron of Honour. I had a cascade of red roses from the florist and wore my hired white dress, long veil and silver sandals. I'd bought a navy blue suit, navy blue shoes and a band of navy blue feathers for a hat to wear as my 'going-away' outfit. We'd booked a week in a B&B (bed and breakfast) in Boscombe for our honeymoon. We had one week's pay each between us, £6 to spend in Bournemouth, and £6 for Mother to look after until we returned so that we

Wedding

could buy food and pay the rent in our new 'digs'. We'd found lodgings locally in a house with a widow and her two teenage children. The rent was 30/- a week. Actually it was just a bedroom and we'd arrange our meals and use of the kitchen and bathroom around the landlady and her family.

Mrs L made a terrible scene during the Service, in fact she wailed like a Banshee, then made a further disturbance when she realised she hadn't been asked to sign the Register as one of the witnesses. When we left the Church I asked her to leave and stay away from the reception and to everyone's relief she went. As my new in-laws were unaware of my background, it must have seemed a very strange carry-on. While I posed for the photographer after the church service, all I could think was 'I don't know this man and I've just promised to spend the rest of my life with him'. I knew that it meant no more flirting and my Mother had told me that if I'd made a mistake don't go back to her. (I think the phrase used was 'You've made your bed so lie on it'.) In those days, when you married it was for life, not until you could be divorced a couple of years down the line if things didn't work out. The reception was prepared by my Mother, she'd been very busy making meat-paste sandwiches and strawberry and jelly trifles in little cardboard dishes (food was still rationed). Mrs L had contributed with the cake. There was a baker in the road where we lived in Salisbury and he'd done us proud, decorating the two-tier cake with anchors and life-belts (very nautical). The only liquid refreshment was cups of tea, my new relatives found the lack of alcohol incredible, though it seemed quite normal to me. The guests from Lincoln were behaving very strangely towards me (and not just because there was no booze) and it was several months later before I learnt the reason. Mrs L had been to each guest in turn to ask how they felt about welcoming a woman from the street into their midst. As they'd only met me briefly before the wedding, I can only imagine what was going through their minds. She behaved true to her rotten character, for hadn't she tried that line before?.

Honeymoon

The B&B in Boscombe was a bit of a shock. On arrival we asked if it was convenient to have a bath, the request didn't go down very well and we couldn't think why. It seemed a reasonable enough question, after all it had been a long tiring day, the wedding, the reception and finally the train journey. Added to all that was the worry of how I would cope as a wife mixed up with the uncertainty of my feelings. When the landlord started to carry buckets of water up the stairs and then repeated the trip until he thought we had enough water for a bath, we realised the work involved. It was a very shallow bath and of course we had to share the same water, but my new spouse was a perfect gentleman and allowed me to bathe first, this gave me the opportunity to be in my new nightie and under the bed covers by the time he emerged from the bathroom. (Like a movie from the 1950s there are no more details of my wedding night!)

Every morning, without fail, we had yellow haddock for breakfast. For the entire duration of our stay it never varied … haddock and a plate of bread and margarine served to us every day. I didn't expect butter as it was rationed, but I'm not a lover of fish and I still thought of it as cat's food. If we'd had dried egg on toast or even a plate of porridge oats it would have made a welcome change. I must confess however to completely ruining the honeymoon. On the Wednesday morning we chanced upon a 'Dutch' auction. A 'very nice man' on the platform seemed to be practically giving the stuff away. All one had to do was be the highest bidder.

'Not five pounds, not four pounds, not even three or two pounds, no not that price, you can have it for a shilling' the man shouted from his platform. 'Easy peasy' I thought.

I made several bids and became the proud owner of six men's handkerchiefs, (useful) an alarm clock and a saucepan, (very very useful) and I'd only spent a shilling. I started to bid for some jewellery and went as high as five pounds (remember the weekly wage was six pounds). I was totally carried away in the excitement and having such fun, I was totally ignoring Larry's warnings. I fell for it hook, line and sinker! The auctioneer took the five pounds. I'd spent all our spare cash on some trashy costume jewellery I didn't like and certainly couldn't afford. (In fact the first thing I did on returning home was to give it to my Bridesmaid, just to forget my embarrassing stupidity.) My new husband was not amused and I could see his point of view. On the Thursday we were hungry and penniless, we sat on a park bench eating fish and chips and pease pudding. We decided to return to Gosport, collect our money from Mother and settle into our new home … Not the most promising start to married life!

I soon sussed out that Larry was only in a good mood if he had his own way and I was extremely adept at finding ways to keep the peace. Money was very tight and I was finding it difficult to find a job. As I was a married woman I wasn't entitled to claim the 'dole'. We both smoked, which at the beginning of each month was not a problem as each sailor was entitled to three hundred 'duty-free' cigarettes, but at the end of the month it was a different matter altogether. I shudder now at what we did. We would put all our 'dog-ends' into a tin and towards the end of each month we would sit at the kitchen table taking them to pieces and re-rolling them into cigarettes, even the landlady was known to 'cadge' one from time to time. Isn't that just too disgusting for words? … good job they weren't tipped cigarettes. We often retired to bed at night feeling hungry, but under the bed we had an untouched tier of wedding cake … we gradually demolished it! My Mother had told me that the top tier of the wedding cake was to be saved for the subsequent Christening of our first child, but when you're young and hungry the important thing is 'now' not 'tomorrow. We were very cramped in our lodgings and privacy was a luxury we didn't enjoy, the landlady even had the grace to tell us about her previous occupants and how the squeaking bed kept her awake at night. Knowing that

Marriage and budgeting

Laundry

... we used the floor! The kitchen arrangement was fraught with problems too; as she had two children her time at the cooker was a priority and I had to fit in whenever I could. Washing was done in the sink (no washing machines or launderettes) and again I had to wait for an appropriate opportunity. I learnt a lesson re-men's pockets and hand-washing. One morning, while Larry was asleep, (he was on night duty at the time) I was washing a navy-blue cardigan of his. Now I knew that wool must be squeezed not wrung and I was doing just that when ... ouch! he'd left a razor blade in the pocket and it had cut through my finger. I went upstairs to ask him to bandage it for me but he was more annoyed at being woken up than concerned about my cut finger! He did promise to check his pockets in future, but no need ... I would be doing that from now on. Not only did I have to wait for my turn to use the kitchen, washing also depended on the weather, there were no spin-driers or synthetic fabrics to assist with drying the clothes and naturally when the weather was good for drying ... the landlady needed the sink and clothes-line!

Gosport Cinemas

We had been married for a few months and I still hadn't managed to find a job. I was finding it difficult to fill in the time during Larry's spells on duty, so I was pleased when my Mother's neighbour asked if I'd like to go to the Cinema with her to see Danny Kaye in *Hans Christian Andersen*. There were two cinemas in Gosport in the 1950s, the 'Forum' and the 'Criterion', the latter having the nickname of 'The fleapit'. The main cinema, The Ritz, was a bombed out shell and the 'Forum' was a temporary cinema until the 'Ritz' could be restored to its former glory. It came near the bottom of priorities to the council, as housing and employment headed the list. Half way through the main feature I became ill, that's an understatement really, I felt as if my whole inside was falling out. Not being promiscuous before marriage I'd never bothered to count the days between periods, when they came they came (I can't believe how naïve I was at the age of twenty). I thought my lack of regularity was because marriage had put my periods out of sync. so to speak. Larry wasn't coming home that night (duty again) so I went to my Mother's house instead of our lodgings and spent the night in the bedroom with my Grandmother. I was in a lot of pain (understatement again) but my Mother stayed downstairs listening to the radio with the volume turned full on, she never once came upstairs to ask how I was feeling. The following morning my Mother had breakfast and left the house for work as usual, but her neighbour, who was worried about me, rang Larry at work to ask him to come home. We had to find a doctor to write out a 'sick certificate' to prove to the Navy that it was a genuine illness, so we walked up the main street and registered at the first surgery we came to. The doctor told me to go home to bed and wait until an ambulance

A miscarriage

arrived to take me to hospital as I'd suffered a miscarriage. We waited all morning, we waited all afternoon, we waited all evening. At nine o'clock Larry went to the phone box to find out what was happening, (still no phones in most houses). They said they were busy and would pick me up as soon as they had an ambulance available. I resigned myself to the fact that they weren't coming that night so I settled down in bed, but whilst listening to Charlie Chaplain's *Limelight* on the radio, the ambulance finally came and I arrived at St Mary's Hospital in Portsmouth at ten o'clock. It took approximately twelve hours from my visit to the doctor to my arrival on the ward!

My hospital stay lasted for two whole weeks, the same blood-stained sheets from an examination on my arrival were still on my bed fourteen days later. The treatment I received consisted of 'Phenol Barbitone' tablets and bed rest. The food was pretty diabolical and my visitors brought me in ham sandwiches and cakes to keep me fed. One afternoon, in my befuddled state, I thought I saw a man doing a 'streak' across the grass, he was being hotly pursued by two nurses carrying blankets and pushing a wheelchair. I turned over and went back to sleep. I told Larry of my dream when he visited in the evening (visiting hours were very strictly controlled in those days), he mentioned it to the nurse and to my relief it wasn't a mirage, a patient had escaped from the mental ward upstairs. I had an added problem on the ward, no way could I sit on a bedpan in full view of the other patients and perform. There were no screens or curtains to give even a hint of decorum, and while I was sitting aloft in full view of everyone, nothing happened. It was decided I'd have a catheter inserted and a jam-jar was placed under my bed to catch the urine. After a couple of days my bottom felt as if I was sitting on red-hot needles, so I asked the nurse if she would do my pressure areas. 'No sign of bed-sores so you don't need any treatment' she replied.

I stupidly thought it was a preventative measure, it seems there's a wide gulf between the things I was taught about nursing and the standard practised here in this hospital. Trying desperately to get some sleep whilst lying on my back and my bottom feeling hotter and hotter, I yanked out the catheter, turned over and slept like a log. There was a lot of 'tutting' next morning because the catheter had 'slipped' out during the night, but I was given a reprieve … if I used the bed pan naturally before the day was out, it wouldn't be replaced. The other women in the ward were marvellous. They ran the taps in the sink by my bed and poured water from one jug to another … zilch! Late that night and with time quickly running out, I was listening to the radio via the head-phones, to Jack Jackson. He would suddenly lower the volume of the music and play a tape of loud foot-steps echoing down a corridor,

'Radios off, Matrons' coming', he would whisper. While I was laughing, nature took it's course, so no more catheter. Larry was angry when he read my notes at the bottom of my bed saying I'd had an abortion and confronted the nurse about it. 'An abortion is anything up to six months' she replied, 'Then it's a miscarriage'

Exactly fourteen days after being admitted to hospital, I was told I could go home. I was informed that I'd been expecting twins and although I'd lost one foetus, the other baby was fine. I had an appointment to visit the ante-natal clinic six weeks later. I hadn't put my feet on the ground since being admitted to hospital and my legs were extremely wobbly and weak. Larry asked if we could have transport back to Gosport but we were told that it would be impossible. We waited for a bus and when it arrived it was standing-room only downstairs. 'No room inside, upstairs only' called the conductor as he rang the bell.

Larry put his hands on my backside to steady me as I attempted the stairs, we then had to catch the harbour ferry and another bus before we finally reached home. Cars were very expensive to buy and definitely not in our income range and a taxi from Portsmouth to Gosport was priced out of the equation. It was a nightmare journey home … and people complain about the Health Service treatment of today!

I received an appointment from the local hospital to see the gynaecologist at two o'clock on a Tuesday afternoon. I arrived ten minutes early as I hate being late. 'Remove your knickers and sit on the bench in the corridor until your name is called' the reception nurse told me. I waited and waited and waited, my name wasn't called. Ladies went into the surgery and ladies came out of the surgery … still I waited. 'What time is your appointment?' I asked the lady sitting next to me. 'Half-past three' she informed me. At three o'clock the nurse carried a tray of tea and biscuits into the doctor's room.

'Okay,' I thought, 'he's had a busy afternoon and entitled to a cup of tea. I could murder a cup myself.' There were no drinks machines in those days so I'd just have to wait until I left the hospital and found a cafe. 'Could you check your list of names to see if I've been forgotten?' I asked the nurse. She checked her notes, 'No', she said, 'You're still on the list, you'll be called as soon as he wants to see you.' The tea tray came out of the room and the half-past three appointment's name was called out. I went into the lavatory, put my knickers on and went home.

The next time I saw a doctor was to see if I was pregnant. My body has a weird way of telling me when I'm expecting, cigarettes make me feel sick, even the smell of tobacco is anathema to me. Lucky for my babies, as it wasn't generally known in the 1950s that smoking could harm the foetus.

A job in an office

As soon as I was back on my feet again I managed to secure a job in an office at one of the MOD (Ministry of Defence) establishments in Gosport, looking after the canteen accounts. I enjoyed the work and the company of the other women. The food was good and because I worked in the office, I ate my lunch with the Manager in the 'Executive' dining room instead of with the other girls in the canteen. We also had a more varied choice of menu. It wasn't long though before I realised I was pregnant. Trying to keep that a secret from all the male customers coming in for their dinner each day was darned near impossible, especially when I was four months into the pregnancy and putting on weight everywhere. I had the task each lunchtime of sitting in a small box with a pile of small change, the canteen girls were not allowed to give change over the counter so the men would bring their money to me, say how much the meal would cost and I would break down their money so that they could tender the correct cost of the meal across the counter. I soon found I was a sitting target for their teasing but I didn't mind, after all I was married and it was legal. The main reason girls didn't get pregnant when they were single was the shame and disgrace it caused. I was married, so it was okay. There wasn't a lot of thought regarding family planning in the 1950s.

I was five months pregnant on my 21st birthday and Larry treated me to a **21st birthday** visit to the theatre and a meal in Southsea. We ate in a small restaurant opposite the Kings Theatre and I remember we ate chicken (which was still considered a special treat), creamed potatoes, carrots and peas before taking our seats in the stalls A farce was showing that week starring Robertson Hare and Moira Lister, I can't swear to this but I think it was called *Dear Father*. Like most farces there were more sub-plots than story, but I remember I laughed a great deal and enjoyed it immensely. My presents for this milestone in my life were mostly practical, i.e. sheets, pillow-cases and towels, plus a few items for the baby. My brother David was on leave from the RAF and Mother made a cake, decorating half of it in pink icing and the other half in blue. We felt like children again, as we used to alternate the day of celebration each year, our birthdays being only one day apart.

I did try very hard to be a good wife, after all I was well schooled in everything domestic. I was expert in keeping house, cleaning, darning socks and although I had a few disasters with my attempts at cake making, the cooking of main meals caused me no problems. I managed to make the house-keeping money last from pay day to pay day. However, to pair up my background with a young man who had problems with his own parents' relationship, was a recipe for disaster one way or another. Larry's emotions were very controlled and I was longing for continuous reassurance that I was loved. I was a tactile person but my husband was the reverse and disliked any signs of affection. He wanted to control me in everything I said and did, it was as suffocating as living with the L's and because of my history I allowed him to dominate ... big mistake on my part! We were desperately short of money and lived in cramped conditions. It was no use complaining though, as lodgings were hard to find especially if the wife was expecting. One week we would use the allotment, an allowance paid to Naval wives over the Post Office counter, and the following week the Navy cash-in hand payment, giving us the princely sum of £6 a week. Food was still rationed, which meant we couldn't overspend on food and one outing a week to the local cinema was about all we could afford.

As soon as the landlady was told of my pregnancy we were given notice to quit so we had to find new lodgings, there were no Naval quarters in the area in the 1950s. Some of the rooms we were offered were really diabolical, landlords taking advantage of a young couple's desperate need to find somewhere to live. One man made a cruel joke at our expense. He told us he had a whole house to let and if we met him at an appointed time outside the property we would have first refusal. We arrived on time but there was no sign of our prospective landlord; when we knocked on the door to enquire what was happening, the elderly owners of the house knew nothing about it. It was a cruel trick to play. We managed to secure 'digs' in the town with a couple who had two young children. We rented the back bedroom and front sitting-room, but again we had to share the kitchen and bathroom with the family. We could only use the bathroom when it suited the resident family and the one toilet was next to the kitchen sink (not much privacy). There was no washing machine and again I could only use the clothes-line if the landlady wasn't using it. As she had two young children and one of them was still in nappies, my washing was done in the evenings and pegged out overnight. Another drawback was the fact that we had to walk through the landlady's sitting room to get to the kitchen. One plus point … the address was nearer to Haslar so Larry didn't have so far to cycle to work. The new address also meant that Larry didn't have to have a supply of pennies in his pocket to pay the toll for crossing Pneumonia Bridge; he'd approach from Alverstoke Village end instead of the Town end. I never quite worked out why the toll was only paid from one direction, perhaps the cost of having a toll-booth both sides of the bridge would have eliminated the profit margins!

We registered for groceries at the corner shop, the butcher in the main street (we still had ration books) and a local coal merchant; we were restricted to the number of bags of coal we could buy, I think it was one hundredweight a month. Each week I paid my wages into the local baby shop to pay for a pram. We'd decided on a 'Pedigree Queen', if my memory serves me right it cost £33. This seemed terribly extravagant on our limited budget but it was the pram with the highest handle that we could find, enabling me to 'pram-push' without having to bend over double each time I walked the baby. The shop was called Keats and they would keep the pram in store until after the birth as it was supposed to be unlucky to have the pram at home before the baby. We did allow ourselves the luxury of a battery radio, but we had to be very selective with our programming, a replacement battery cost 12/-! We made certain we had enough 'power' on Sundays to listen in to Pete Murray's *Top Twenty Show* on Radio Luxembourg. Our favourite record at this time was *Cherry Pink and Apple-Blossom White* by the Man with the Golden Trumpet, Eddy Calvert. The way he'd slide those notes turned my stomach over … it was great!

In the winter of 1953/4 we had some heavy snow falls. All the buses were cancelled, but we were still expected to get to work on time. Every morning between six thirty and seven there was a convoy of workers walking along the Fareham road to reach the MOD establishments where they were employed. We had to 'clock-in' on arrival and if we were five minutes late we would lose fifteen minutes pay … regardless of the reason for being late.

There was also a lot of camaraderie between the commuters and the bus-conductors in the early mornings. I can remember running for a bus and being jollied along by the conductor, 'Come on, come on, we're all waiting to go to work', he would shout from the platform as he waved his arms for us to hurry.

One morning, during the early stages of pregnancy, I slipped on some mud and fell flat onto my back-side, I saw the funny side of it and just laughed as I sat there in such a ridiculous position. My mackintosh was covered in dirt so I had to return home to change my clothes. Larry was still in bed as I entered the house, he didn't start work until an hour after me. He was furious when I told him why I needed clean clothes; telling him I'd laughed as I sat in the mud didn't help the situation. To be honest what else can you do but laugh when you land on your bum in a muddy field? … no sense of humour that man! The next morning the bus conductor and passengers applauded when I stepped onto the bus, they'd heard me laughing and my Mother (she travelled with me each morning to a different establishment but in the same direction) had explained what had happened.

The cost of vegetables was very cheap, potatoes were only a penny a pound and for a shilling I could buy enough vegetables to make a nourishing stew, oxtail being a favourite. Larry was having a re-think about meat. We would buy 'wether mutton' for a Sunday joint, it was very tough if not cooked slowly, or a stuffed and rolled neck of lamb, giving the flavour of a roast dinner without the substance. Our first Christmas together as a married couple was in 1953, my Father-in-law sent us a leg of pork through the post; it was an excellent postal service in those days. Larry brought home a chicken from a colleague at work, it was still warm and had all its feathers intact. We plucked it okay but Larry baulked at the idea of placing his hands inside the warm interior to clean it out … a doddle after skinning rabbits! (I knew it would come in useful one day.) **Domestic life**

One morning I took delivery of a parcel from Lincoln and as I slowly unwrapped it the smell emanating from it was really awful. It was a pheasant, resplendent in all it's plumage. I plucked it but couldn't bring myself to eat it, despite Larry's assurances that game had to hang and be 'high' before being eaten. My nose was too close to my mouth and the stench was intermixed with my taste buds … uuugh! **Pheasant to cook**

One evening Larry asked if he could take my stamp collection to work; one of his mates was a keen philatelist and when he was told of my album he showed great interest in seeing some of my pre-war stamps. I said it was okay and the next morning Larry took the album to Haslar. I never saw my stamps again, Larry had sold the whole collection for a measly ten shillings (fifty pence). I was devastated, but Larry pointed out that ten shillings was more useful than little squares of paper. To me it was the final link to the past with my Father, but the deal had been made and there was absolutely nothing I could do about it. The buyer had an exceptional piece of good fortune as some of the stamps were extremely rare.

We often had a treat on Saturdays from the local fish-monger. I don't like **Fish**

fish but I did enjoy hard cod's-roe deep fried in batter, or a pint of prawns which we would eat out of the paper, sitting at the table and heading and tailing them with great relish. I had a terribly sweet tooth, probably due to lack of choco-late and biscuits during the war, however I could buy broken biscuits by the pound, enough to last us for a whole week. The grocery shop in Gosport High Street would display a row of tins outside their premises full of broken biscuits and we just helped ourselves; mind you the chocolate-coated biscuits were always eaten first. I think my favourite treat was Brazil nut toffee from Wool-worths. The shop assistant would have a small toffee hammer and break enough toffee from the tin tray to the correct weight. If I could I would have bought the whole tray. It's no wonder I had trouble with my teeth, but during my preg-nancy I couldn't get enough of this confectionery. The only other craving I remember was for beetroot, I would cook it but never managed to slice it and put it into vinegar without my hand going on automatic pilot to my mouth!

We had a few tense moments every Navy pay day (once a fortnight). With-out fail Larry's friend, who was still single, would call and ask him to go to the pub for a drink. As I was pregnant he always declined, there just wasn't any spare cash. It created a very strained atmosphere and my beloved was a class 'A' sulker! Larry was almost paranoid about contracting Polio, it seemed to be the disease that was most prevalent now that T.B. was finally under control. The thought of spending one's life in an 'Iron-Lung' was really frightening and every time he had even the slightest sore throat he seemed convinced he'd caught Polio. One morning Larry awoke with a sore throat and a rash had appeared on the upper part of his body, he asked me to ring the hospital to say he wouldn't be able to go to work that day. I went out to the nearest telephone kiosk and asked the hospital to send someone to see him, explaining that as I was pregnant I was worried the baby could be harmed if it was anything infec-tious. An ambulance arrived within ten minutes and whisked him away to hos-pital. Larry stayed in the ward for twenty-four hours and was then told to go back on duty as he was fine and only had a heat rash. He was very angry when he came home (embarrassed really) but as I explained I didn't want to endan-ger the baby's life. He calmed down ... but never mentioned Polio again.

In the Spring of 1954 we travelled to Lincoln to stay with my in-laws (yes, I took toilet paper with me). It was while I was shopping with the aunt that I was told about the conversations with Mrs L during our wedding. I felt terri-ble, but the aunt said not to worry they thought she was mad. During our stay we went to Nottingham to the theatre, top of the bill was Semprini. When he came on stage he'd say: 'Old ones, new ones, loved ones, neglected ones' as an introduction to his performance in those gentle tones so familiar to radio lis-teners. His repertoire didn't disappoint the audience, he played the piano beautifully and with feeling. Jon Pertwee was also on the bill, the curtain rose to show an empty stage, the lights went down, the audience was hushed wait-ing in anticipation ... nothing happened. Suddenly a rope was thrown down

Groceries

A health scare

Nottingham

from the fly and Jon slid down it to land on centre stage, he was dressed in a bright green suit and proceeded to entertain everyone with his jokes and silly accents. What an entrance though, one that's hard to forget!

We put our names on the local housing list, but we didn't qualify for a house unless we had two children, preferably one of each sex. We'd have to wait. Buying our own house never entered the equation, we'd need a mortgage for at least a thousand pounds, and we needed ten percent of the purchase price as a deposit. How could we save up a hundred pounds when we could only just manage from week to week? … it was as likely as a man going to the moon! I wished at times that the pre-fabs were still standing, they would have been ideal starter-homes for young couples, but they were erected as a stop-gap on the understanding that they only had a ten year 'life' and the tenants were to be re-housed as soon as brick houses became available.

I had now finished work and was attending monthly ante-natal clinics at the local maternity home, husbands were not invited or expected to attend. I count myself very fortunate to have experienced child-birth at 'The Blake Maternity Home'. There were only two wards and the staff and atmosphere were wonderful. Husbands were considered non-entities and as far as the staff were concerned they'd done their bit, the rest was up to the women. This was considered exclusively a womens' domain and was nothing to do with the male of the species. The monthly visits included a medical and a 'Hello' from your GP, our blood-pressure was checked and urine tested to ensure everything was as it should be. We were shown pictures of a foetus in its various stages of development, learnt to pant, use the gas and air machine and do some exercises. It was more reassuring than anything else and a chance to know the midwife and meet other mothers.

Blake Maternity Home

I had to smile one day, I was lying on a bed waiting for the doctor, when I heard loud sobbing coming from the adjoining cubicle. 'I've changed my mind' cried the young 'mum-to-be'. 'Isn't the baby due next week?' asked the doctor. 'But I don't want it' cried the distraught young girl. 'Where's your husband?' asked the doctor. 'He's away on his ship' she wailed. 'Well' said the doctor 'It's too late to change your mind now, you'll just have to give birth'. I was trying to think what alternative the young wife had in mind at this late stage in her pregnancy! My doctor told me afterwards, 'She's away from her family and the other naval wives on the estate had frightened her with all their old wives tales, she'll be okay though'.

I was very fortunate with my pregnancy, I'm one of those women who 'bloom', even my hair shone. Maternity clothes were not the most well designed outfits of the day, I had a skirt with an adjustable waistband and several brightly coloured smocks. The women's magazines of the day advocated disguising the 'bump' and drawing the eye to the upper part of the body, hence the attractive smocks. Coats in the 1950s were called 'swaggers' which meant they were very loose, especially at the back, where they literally 'swaggered'

Maternity clothes

... hence the name. Unfortunately, I was due to give birth in August so I couldn't disguise my shape with my coat. (I don't believe I've just written 'disguise', but that's exactly what we were supposed to do, maybe that's why I can't honestly remember seeing a pregnant woman whilst I was growing up ... they were all disguised!)

I enjoyed the times when my brother, Gerald, came home on leave especially as my Mother was at work and Larry on duty. One day we decided to go to Portsmouth to the cinema, he insisted we walk arm in arm even though I was heavily pregnant; I think he thought I was top heavy and was likely to fall flat on my face. He looked very smart in his Merchant Navy Officer's uniform as we strolled to the pontoon to catch the ferry across the harbour. We laughed like a couple of school kids when the usherette guided us to the courting couple seats, these were double seats with no arm rest in between. When Larry came home that evening he couldn't wait to tell me about a phone call he'd received at work.

'One of the staff rang me today, she asked, "Do you know your wife is having an affair behind your back.? I saw her in the High Street with an officer, flaunting herself with no sense of shame, and in her condition ... disgusting". I thanked her and said I would confront you when I got home.' What a mischief-making bitch! Pardon my French!

Like all good babies mine decided to arrive in the middle of the night and at the weekend. None of the things I had been told actually happened, no 'show' or the 'breaking of waters', I just 'threw up'. I awoke Larry and asked him to phone for a taxi. The nearest phone box was a ten minute walk away so I dressed, picked up my suitcase and waited at the front gate for his return. I remember thinking what a lovely night it was, the moon and stars were shining in a cloudless sky, I was amazingly calm. The taxi arrived and when we reached the maternity home the driver said: 'Good Luck, have this trip on me.' Aren't people kind?

New baby

Despite my haste to reach the 'Blake' it was nearly twenty-four hours later at ten minutes to midnight when my daughter decided to enter the world. I think 'WOW' sums up my first reaction as I held her in my arms; the emotions I experienced were unbelievable, the intensity of the feelings nearly ripped my heart and stomach in two, I was completely overwhelmed by the strength of it all. I knew there and then that nobody would ever hurt this girl, she would be protected by me from anyone who would try to hurt her or take her from me. I also promised I would do my utmost to make this marriage work so that she could grow up in a safe and secure home. A 'mother hen' couldn't have been more protective. I also knew for certain, that whatever the future held I would never be separated from my child. We named her Sally, which means Princess, and Jane, meaning God's gift.

The nursing of new mothers was very strict. We were not allowed out of bed for six days and on the seventh day we were only allowed to 'sit out' for tea in the ward, we were not discharged until the fourteenth day. It sounds very o.t.t.(over the top) by today's standards but we returned home feeling less frightened of how to handle the new baby and well and truly rested. I learnt a new word. Two or three times a day a ward maid would come into the room saying, 'Anyone for bunnies?'

I kept saying 'No thankyou' as I didn't know what she meant. Meanwhile Larry was complaining about the expense of having to buy numerous packets of sanitary towels. I mentioned this to one of the patients. 'They're free, why don't you ask for some when the ward maid comes on her 'bunny-round?' she said: So that's what bunnies are … silly me!

Matron demonstrated many times that babies were not as fragile as we thought, she would open the ward door carrying as many as four babies at a time, balancing them on her knees as she struggled with the door-handles. If baby was fast asleep at feeding time she would unwrap the tiny bundle and stretch the small arms and legs, sort of 'press-ups' lying on their backs. I even

Matron knows best

watched open-mouthed one day when she held a baby upside down by its ankles to wake it up! No, she wasn't cruel, she instilled a confidence in the new mums before they returned home to manage on their own. The babies didn't sleep by the side of the Mother's bed they slept in the nursery. For the first seven days we only held our babies at feeding-time. On the eighth day we were shown how to change the nappies and bathe baby, learning to care for them before returning home. The food in the 'home' was excellent, fresh fruit and vegetables every day, meat and fish all beautifully cooked and presented. 'How can you feed baby if you're under nourished yourself'. Matron would say.

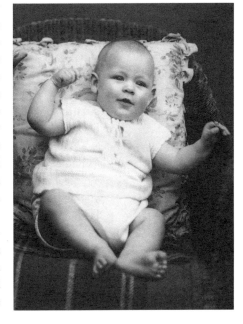

Visitors were restricted, it was husbands only, no parents or other relatives Visiting hours were only from seven o'clock until eight o'clock each evening and an hour on Saturday and Sunday afternoon … new mums needed plenty of rest. I know that I personally appreciated the time to learn how to handle a baby, I'd only held one baby before and that was my niece at her Christening. I was sad when I left the home, it was the best time of my life with the added bonus of my little girl to cuddle and hug whenever I wanted … sheer bliss.

Money was now tighter than before and Larry gave me a small book in which I was required to account for every penny I spent. One day I was 3d. out and it was a while before I remembered I'd bought an ice-cream in Woolworths!

The pram

I loved my pram and pushed it with pride but Sally was one of those babies who swallowed eight ounces of milk and threw back three, so a Terry nappy was always covering the white satin pillow-case. When we visited friends I would ask for newspapers to be placed on the floor when she had a feed as I now knew that as soon as I started to 'wind' her she would start to 'pump' back the contents of her stomach! I didn't make any milk myself, this was a huge disappointment to me, but we could buy a milk substitute from the Government at a subsidised price. When I took Sally to the doctor because I was worried she may not be having enough nourishment he suggested I try different brands to find one that suited her digestive system. The one that finally suited her was the most expensive on the market. That's my girl, start as you mean to go on! We were also given free bottles of orange-juice concentrate for babies, it smelt awful but they seemed to enjoy it.

Washing was a nightmare! I could only use the sink and washing line if the landlady wasn't using it for her clothes, which was not very often as she also had a husband and two young children. The baby clothes were wool, cotton or 'Vyella' and drying them took ages. All the laundry was done by hand and the woollens could only be squeezed and not wrung, so it needed either hot sun or a good wind to dry them. Add to this the piles of Terry nappies, my husband's white naval shirts and starched collars, bed and cot linen … I had a washing and drying problem!

Two months after Sally's birth I still hadn't started menstruating so I thought I'd better visit the doctor to find out when my menstrual cycle should start again. He gave me three pills and said come back and see him if nothing happened. Nothing happened. I returned to the doctor.

'You're putting on a bit of beef, I think you're pregnant again' he said after examining me. I must have had an expression of horror and disbelief on my face as he started to laugh. 'Last year you thought you were barren for life and now you wish you were!' he said.

I failed to see the humour in either of his remarks! Larry was not pleased. Had I missed something here? … why was it all my fault? I told my Mother, she told me I was silly to be pregnant again. Not that my husband had anything to do with it … just me. I was scared, I thought I would be like a rabbit having a baby every year. I was worried about money and our living conditions and the general consensus of opinion seemed to suggest that I was the irresponsible one. I felt very isolated and miserable but I would cuddle Sally as there were no recriminations coming from her.

We went to the council to see if we could improve our living conditions, but they were adamant, 'Come back when you have two children'. 'I'm pregnant now, can't we have a house before the next baby arrives?' I pleaded. 'No, if you have two children of the same sex you will be allocated a two-bedroom property, but if you have one of each then you will have a three-bedroom house'. We'd just have to wait, but at least it looked hopeful.

I was not 'blooming' with my second pregnancy, I hadn't lost much weight from my first pregnancy and now I was piling on the pounds, my muscles had not bounced back and I looked as if the baby had 'dropped' from about the fourth month. I wore my coat most of the time to try to disguise the fact that I was expecting again while I still had a young baby in the pram. I went to the ante-natal clinic and the midwife told me off for starting another baby so soon after giving birth. 'You're not being fair', she said. 'Your new baby will be undernourished as you haven't given your body enough time to build itself up again.'

Pregnant again

I was feeling bad enough without her telling me I would also do my new baby harm! It was a long hot summer. I was huge, uncomfortable and frightened that my baby would be born undernourished. Larry had the look of a man trapped, he was not happy. The saving ray of sunshine was our daughter, she was a delight in every way and my 'bump' was a convenient place to balance her when I was busy. I had a large playpen in our room where she could play safely while I was in the kitchen, the 'nappy' filled string lines a permanent fixture strung across the room. Trying to get them dried and aired didn't bother her a jot, she was a most contented baby.

Aunt Ellen and Uncle Ben lived nearby. They now had five children which meant I had three cousins I didn't know existed before. Aunt Ellen was a kind lady and would give me piles of baby clothes that she had kept from her last baby. She also gave us a cot which was made of iron, painted green and had brass knobs at each corner. This cot was in stark contrast to Sally's which was a present from her Grandfather in Lincoln; it was the most up-to-date item of nursery furniture with polished wood bow ends and decorated with nursery motifs.

We still had our weekly outing to the 'Forum'. Mother would look after Sally in the evening after she'd returned from work. We asked her if she would baby-sit one Sunday and she was horrified to think we would want to go to the cinema on the Sabbath! I was pleased to see that a film had been made of Richard Gordon's *Doctor in the House* and looked forward to a 'good drool' over the leading man, Dirk Bogart. It was during the film that we decided to call our next baby Simon. I don't know what the outcome would have been be if I had another daughter! ... stick an 'e' on the end I suppose.

The Forum

One of the more noticeable fears nowadays is not being able to leave the pram and baby outside shops. I never gave it a second thought that anyone would hurt or take a child from its pram. All the new mums would put the brakes on their prams, do their shopping and return outside the shop to find everything as they'd left it. Sally would say 'Dada' to every man in uniform that passed by, which caused a few embarrassed smiles and pink cheeks. There was also a great deal of respect for expectant women, nobody, male, female or child would dream of keeping their seat on the bus leaving a pregnant lady to stand. I've actually seen a bus conductor tell a child off for not automatically giving up his seat. The grocer who we'd registered with would often put his hand under the counter and produce a tin of fruit or some other delicacy that was in short supply that he'd saved for us. One day he offered us a tin of oysters, neither of us had tasted them before so we were looking forward to eating them for our tea, … no! we couldn't swallow them. I hadn't tasted them before and I certainly can't understand why they're a luxury.

Larry was on summer leave and had decided to visit his relatives in Lincoln, leaving me at my Mother's in case the baby arrived while he was away. Mother was at work during the day but my brother was on leave from the Merchant Navy. Sally was staying with my sister who now had a council house in Wilton, and we would collect Sally after the new baby had arrived. I enjoyed the company of my brother, I didn't want him to panic if the baby started so to put him at his ease, I said just ring for a taxi if the pains start and I'll be okay. 'I know what to do if the baby arrives, sit it between your legs and wait for the doctor to cut the umbilical cord', he said: My baby brother was not a baby anymore, he'd learnt what to do while training to be an officer.

Larry had returned from his leave and was back at work but still no sign of labour pains, so each morning I waddled to my Mother's house and spent the day in my brother's company. One morning, it was thundering and lightning and I fancied scrambled eggs, but while I was in the kitchen my contractions started. Gerald phoned for a taxi and I was on my way to the Blake while he contacted my husband to let him know the baby was on its way. The usual procedure of bath, enema and an examination on arrival had been completed and I was safely tucked up in bed. 'As it's lunch-time we'll leave you with a buzzer and see you after I've eaten', said the midwife.

This was not going to take as long as Sally's birth, the pains were much more intense. The midwife suddenly appeared. 'I had this feeling that you might need me before I finished my lunch. I think we'd better get you into the labour ward as soon as we can', she said. She was right and Simon (means Awakening) Geoffrey (meaning Peace) entered the world half an hour later.

This baby that they assured me would be underweight and undernourished weighed nine and a half pounds!

Larry in trouble   There was quite a commotion in the corridor at visiting time, I could hear Matron tearing a strip off some poor soul … it was Larry. He arrived very sunburnt and carrying a bunch of flowers. He'd spent the afternoon at the beach, swimming and sun-bathing and generally having a good time. He'd been with my Mother and one of her friends, the flowers were from the friend's garden, which explained why he'd brought them as I didn't get flowers when I had Sally. Matron pounced on him as soon as he arrived through the door, 'Where have you been all afternoon while your wife was giving birth to your son?' she asked. 'I've been to the beach. The first baby took hours and I didn't think this one would be here yet,' he replied. 'Well, you were wrong', she said. 'It wouldn't have hurt you to pick up a telephone to find out would it?' He was humbled and looked very sheepish as he walked towards my bed. I don't think Matron had a very high opinion of fathers!

I was becoming increasingly worried about Simon, the Matron insisted I feed him myself but he inevitably returned to the nursery crying, whereas all the other babies were completely knocked out and sated. Mothers will understand when I say I could hear him crying in the nursery. When my GP paid me his courtesy visit after the first week he asked me why I was so glum and when I explained that my baby seemed hungry all the time. 'Don't worry,' he said. 'The nurse feeds him with a bottle once the other babies have been settled down.'

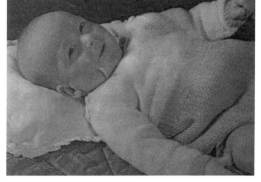

A lot of heartache would have been spared if someone had thought to tell me! After fourteen days I returned home and the first task ahead was to buy new baby clothes as none of the first-size garments would fit Simon, even a pair of white satin baby shoes, which were so pretty I couldn't resist buying them, were never worn.

Mother went to Wilton to collect Sally, I couldn't believe how much she'd grown in the four weeks she'd been away. I was reduced to tears when I bathed her in the evening as she cried 'Mum, mum' and she didn't mean me, she had grown accustomed to my sister feeding her and putting her to bed. Simon was born exactly one month and three days before Sally's first birthday. I was told they were called 'Irish Twins' as once a year they were both the same age.

It was now imperative we call in at the Housing Department to see if we had enough points to qualify for a house of our own. Firstly they would need to inspect our living conditions. I informed the landlady that someone from the Council would be visiting and would want to look at the kitchen and bathroom as well as our rooms. When the woman saw the toilet next to the kitchen she was visibly shocked.

'No way can you stay here with two babies. It's now July and the Council is on holiday during August but I promise you I will put in your application at the first housing meeting in September,' she said. On the first Monday in September the lady from the Council was at the door. 'Have you got 10/- you can spare to buy a key; there's a brand new house waiting for you to move into and the first rent payment isn't due until next Monday.' 'Can I have 10/-?' I asked Larry as soon as he came through the door. 'What for?' he replied. I was enjoying the moment as he obviously thought I'd overspent on something. 'To buy a key from the Council, we have a house', I almost yelled at him in my excitement.

A new home

We collected the key and were like two children in a sweet factory, we couldn't believe how lucky we were, a place to ourselves, magic! I must mention that Gosport Council was true to its word; they had said that at the first meeting in September after their summer break, they would consider our application for housing and here we were with a key on the second Monday of the month ... well done Gosport council. Tuesday afternoon we went to inspect our new home armed with a broom, dustpan and brush, bucket, scrubbing brush and soap. We cleaned and scrubbed the house from top to bottom eliminating all the signs of the builders. It looked very bare but we were so thrilled and excited we didn't care, it was to be our very own home. Our first purchase was curtain material for all the windows which we took to my Mother who made up curtains on her 'Singer' sewing machine. I don't think she had much sleep that night. Our next task was to find some furniture so we went to a local furniture shop, Abrahams, on the corner of Spring Garden Lane and Stoke Road. We could only afford the bare necessities so we bought two twin beds, one large rug, two easy chairs, a red formica draw-leaf table and four black metal dining chairs covered in red plastic. That was all we could buy with the money we'd scraped together. The reason we bought twin divan beds instead of a double bed was that we could put the mattresses on the floor to sleep on when we had visitors, our guests could then sleep on the bases. We decided we might as well move on Wednesday instead of waiting until the weekend, so arranged for the furniture to be delivered then.

The van driver said, 'If you can be ready at eight o'clock in the morning I'll collect you and your bits and pieces and take you with me when I deliver your order.'

Great! Mind you, getting two babies ready that early was going to be a struggle but I was too excited to sleep anyway. I told the landlady our plans and just like Queen Victoria ... she was not amused. I explained that we had a house and surely in similar circumstances she would prefer to move as soon as possible, we had paid our rent up to the end of the week so she wasn't losing money. She wanted a week's notice. This was frightening, as no way could we pay her and the Council out of one week's pay. Her answer to our dilemma was to keep our coal in lieu of notice. I don't think I've ever forgiven her for that as our month's coal allowance for September was already there, plus we'd built up our stock of fuel from the summer's quota, but we had Hobson's choice ... coal or money. No choice at all! Most of what we owned went into the two cots and early that Wednesday morning, Larry and I, carrying a baby each, climbed up beside the van driver, our meagre belongings and new bits of furniture safely in the back of the van. We set out to start afresh in our brand new home on the new council estate at Rowner.

We were very proud of our bits and pieces although they didn't quite add up to a fully furnished home. We knew we had plenty of time to add things if and when we could afford them. The rent was a bit of a lottery, the Council charged according to the husband's income. The Navy pay was announced each year in the Portsmouth Evening News so our income was known to all and sundry. We had neighbours earning more money each week than we did and paying less rent, as the bulk of their pay-packet was made up by working 'overtime' and they only had to declare their flat rate of pay for assessment. When we had a pay rise of £1 a week the rent increased by 7/6d! We thought it a bit unfair, but it was the rules and we were just grateful to have a house.

The next item we bought was a sideboard. and the way we saved up for the deposit was by shopping at the local Co-op and saving up our 'divi'. If you were a 'member' you would receive a 'dividend' slip with each purchase made and at the end of the year you'd stick the slips onto a form, the Co-op would then pay out a percentage, or 'divi' in cash. We were very grateful to a friend of my Mothers for buying us a £1 share which made us members. She did this when she heard the story about the coal and it was a God-send. It worked like this: as a member we could order £5 worth of coal and pay it back at 5/- a week for 20 weeks, this meant we could have a fire without the fear of running out of fuel before the coalman's next delivery. With two babies in the house it was essential we had the where-with-all to keep warm. We had three bedrooms which were extremely empty, two only having a cot in the centre of the room and the third, our twin beds. The floor-boards were bare as we hadn't enough cash to buy lino. We made bedside tables and cupboards from tea-chests which I'd disguise with material to give the impression they were proper pieces of furniture. Larry bought some chip-board and worked hard at making corner units for the living room, they were painted black (always looked dusty) but must have been sturdily made for they were finally disposed of 40 years later! Our bedroom rug was quite unique, it was the reason for all the requests for odd thrums of wool, the design was abstract, but there were pink hearts in several places and in the border were my initials (and it was made before we were married). The rug was finally put on the 'tip' in 1999. The moths had discovered it tucked in a cupboard and made a proper meal out of it. Shame really, because it still had a lot of wear in it. We had a mat in the kitchen which was really hard to make. We asked the local green-grocer for a potato sack and scrounged old coats, jackets and skirts from everyone we knew. I would sit in the evenings cutting up the discarded clothes into thin strips of material ... lots of blisters on my fingers from the scissors! Larry would weave the strips into the potato sack making a colourful and serviceable mat for the kitchen.

I found I had a gruelling routine to contend with and very little time for pleasure. Sally didn't walk until she was 18 months old, was still in nappies and

Furniture

A mother's routine

on a normal regime for her meals. Simon was still on four hourly feeds and also in nappies. Larry expected a cooked breakfast before leaving the house at half past seven each morning and the house to be clean and tidy when he returned in the evening for his dinner. The floors were made of brown Marley tiles and needed polishing every day, even then a thin film of dust would appear by mid-afternoon. I would start my day at half past five in the morning so that I could do some washing and cleaning before the babies awoke, fortunately for me they were happy contented children, otherwise I think I would have gone round the twist.

My first outing to the shops with two babies was a disaster. We'd bought a seat to put at the end of the pram for Sally, but when I put on the brake outside the shop the pram started to tip forward, there was nothing else to do but carry her while I bought my groceries. I'd noticed twin boys, about four years old, playing in a garden on my way to the Co-op and a twin pram with a small baby sleeping in it. I wondered.

Nothing ventured, nothing gained so they say, so I knocked on the door to see if we could do a straight swap, her twin pram for my single pram. The lady was hesitant at first, I think she thought I was mad. 'My pram is four years old and yours is almost brand new, it wouldn't be fair,' she protested. 'But my pram is useless to me, it tips when both babies are in it,' I explained.

When she finally realised I was serious she agreed to the exchange. Her sleeping son was transferred to the Pedigree Queen and my two infants were placed in the large, brown twin carriage. That evening her husband knocked on the door with a twin push-chair and two pairs of walking reins, he said his wife insisted I should have them to make it all fair and to seal the bargain. Every baby

should have a pram designed like that twin pram. When it rained there were two flaps and two hoods to keep the occupants dry and sheltered from the wind, while under the mattress there was a cavity that ran the length of the pram, I could put spare nappies and food in the pram's base if I wanted to go out visiting for the day. It was a super pram and the day I knocked at that door was surely a lucky day for me.

Visiting the in-laws

Larry's first leave period after Simon's birth meant another trip to Lincoln to show off our new arrival to his relatives. I'd already upset my Father-in-law by not calling the baby Geoffrey. He insisted that the first male of the family always had that name. I met him half way and Geoffrey became Simon's second name. They'd already met Sally when we took her to Lincoln at the ripe old age of six weeks to be christened.

When we left the train at Waterloo I refused to go on the tube train with the babies; I had visions of the doors closing on the carry-cot as they had done previously on the grip. I wasn't going to have my baby sliced in two by a train door, so I insisted we hail a taxi. The cab driver sat at the wheel while we put two babies, luggage and carry-cot into his cab and when we reached Paddington he sat there while we reversed the process. My husband paid him the exact fare. 'Where's my tip?' he asked. 'No tip,' my beloved replied.

What happened next was a nightmare! The driver leapt out of his cab (I was surprised to see he did actually have a pair of legs!) 'I'll tell every cab driver for miles around what you're like. You won't ever get another London cab to accept your fare,' he shouted at our retreating backs. We slunk away wishing we could disappear down a hole! Luckily the rest of the journey was straight forward.

'Hello Geoff' said my Father-in-law as he took the baby from me. 'His name is Simon,' I growled, I was going to win this point if it was the last thing I'd do. 'Now you have a pigeon pair there's no need to have anymore,' said the Aunt , 'Once you have one of each there's no need to try for another.' Why was everyone trying to tell me how to live my life? I thought having babies was the best experience in the world, they were warm, cuddly and returned my love without question. Hard work? Yes, but they gave so much in return. I was glad when the time came to return home. We avoided both the underground and the taxis, we travelled across London by bus … it was a lot cheaper and we had a tour of London at the same time, much less stressful!

The fashions in the late 1950s were very feminine and after eighteen months of pregnancy I was enjoying my new found figure … I had a waist! So okay I also had hips, but the new fashion was ideal for my shape. American teenagers (now that was a new word for us) wanted to Bee-bop, (the latest dance craze) and their skirts were very full with layers of frilly petticoats underneath; as the girls 'bopped' their skirts would swing and swirl around showing their petticoats in all their glory. The only problem with this fashion was that the petticoats cost more than a skirt and to get the best effect you needed at least three! When not being worn they wouldn't fit into the wardrobe so they would hang in vain glory on hangers suspended from the picture rail. Now why don't fashion designers and interior decorators work together because it was now the 'done thing' to take down the picture rails to give an impression of higher ceilings.

**Larry's
qualifications**

Larry had second thoughts about leaving the Navy and decided to stay until he'd served twelve years; maybe the added responsibilities had something to do with his decision. He had a far-seeing boss at the time who was interested enough in Larry's career to encourage him to take some O-levels, so every evening he would study Maths and English ... he passed. He was now qualified to study for his Mental Nurse qualifications, (RMN), and to achieve this he would train at St. James hospital in Portsmouth for three years. It was a strange period, we were still a 'Service' family but Larry wore civilian clothes. We were still paid by the Navy and he received his 300 duty-free cigarettes each month, but our social circle was with civilian nurses and not service personnel. The hours were strange, all of the duties were shifts and the hours he worked varied from day to day. Another nurse's wife told me to keep a chart otherwise I would never get the hang of it. Larry's day off would be one day later each week so that the only time he had a week-end free was when his day off fell on a Saturday one week and Sunday the next, once every six weeks ... they were extremely long shifts. Larry would ride a bicycle to Portsmouth each day, crossing the Harbour by ferry. He did try the new invention of a motorised back wheel on his bike at one stage, but the weight of the motor was not cost effective as the back tyre needed renewing too frequently.

Gerald had now married and was about to emigrate to New Zealand, I was saddened by this as we were just beginning to get to know each other. He stayed in the Merchant Navy until he gained his 'Master's Ticket', but he'd been working on ships for the 'New Zealand Shipping Company' and liked the opportunities he'd seen in that young country. He would be away from home for six months at a time which was not what is most desirable to a young couple of newly-weds. During his visits to Australia and New Zealand he'd made a lot of friends but preferred the latter country of the two. One good thing came from his leaving the Country ... he gave us his Lambretta, it made a huge difference to Larry's journey to and from work, it was quick and cheap to run. Gerald said it would compensate for all the Christmas and birthday presents he was bound to forget!

I was gradually growing into the routine of life as a wife and mother, not a great deal of time to think but the days seemed to slip by very quickly. All my neighbours were young parents like ourselves, setting up home for the first time. The kitchen became a focal point for morning tea or coffee, although coffee was not very common in the 1950s. Its lack of popularity could be partly due to the taste of the only available coffee at the time ....Camp coffee, it was a liquid in a ketchup-shaped bottle and only bore a slight resemblance to the real thing. Our only entertainment was gossip and the radio. During the morning I would tune into the Medium Wave station of the BBC to listen to *House-wife's Choice*, followed by *Mrs. Dale's Diary* and *Music While You Work*. During the afternoon I'd hear all the useful hints and cookery tips from Women's Hour and when the weather was too bad to take the children for a walk in their pram, I would enjoy the excellent productions of *The Afternoon Play*. The highlight of each evening's listening was *The Archers*. I can remember clearly the night Christine Archer was burnt to death in her stables. When I think about it now I realise what sad lives we led. That particular evening the man from the Pru. (Prudential Insurance) called for his weekly payment. We sat in the living room in absolute silence, even he whispered as if a death had taken place in the family and not that of a fictional character on the radio! We kept the wireless turned off for the remainder of that evening out of respect for Grace, we felt so upset ... incredible!

My main hobby was knitting, every evening I had a pair of needles perma- **Knitting** nently clicking from dinner-time to bed-time. The small local shop would put the wool 'by' so that I could buy an ounce at a time or when money permitted. I found it the only way to dress the children as I wanted, new children's clothes being expensive. I would knit two of every pattern as I liked to dress the children in identical outfits. Jumpers were no problem, for cardigans I only had to change the side of the button-holes and buttons and when I knitted a skirt for Sally I would knit a pair of short trousers for Simon in the same colour wool. Although they were called 'Irish Twins' Simon was quickly catching his sister up in size. A friend of a friend worked at the 'Ladybird' factory in Portsmouth and the staff often had the opportunity to buy 'seconds' at a greatly reduced price. One evening she called round with two camel duffle coats and tartan trews and I couldn't find a single fault to class them as 'seconds'. The linings of the coats matched the tartan of the trews, I bought two yellow sweat-shirts to complete the outfit ... they looked very smart. There was a slight drawback with the yellow sweatshirts though, because of the bright colour they could only be worn for a short while before going into the wash and the average drying time was three days! Still no washing machine or spin-dryer. We did have a gas boiler though and it was invaluable for the nappies, bed-linen and Larry's white shirts, but the majority of baby clothes had to be hand-washed. A new wool came on the market ... nylon, only here again it was a matter of three hours' wear and three days' drying-time!

A new breed of salesman started to call on the estate offering free demon- **Salesmen** strations with his 'Rolls Washing Machine'. Now I had already learnt that I was not to buy things on 'tick' at the door. When we first moved into our new home I bought a set of copper-bottomed saucepans at the door; the full cost was three pounds and I was well pleased with the purchase at only three shillings a week for ten weeks. When Larry came home from work and I proudly showed him my pots he was furious with me and made me promise never ever to buy from salesmen at the door again. He paid the three pounds off in one go. We went very short of luxuries like sweets or biscuits for several weeks until I'd made up the shortfall. I was a fast learner ... lesson learnt! However, he seemed to think it a good idea to have the 'Rolls' man come round one evening to do our washing, especially as we insisted at the outset that no-way could we afford one of his machines. We had blankets, nappies, sheets, curtains and anything else we could think of to let this poor man do our laundry. He washed everything, we made him cups of tea, we chatted about anything and everything as soon as he started his sales pitch. 'I give up', he said, 'I cannot get going on my sales pitch and I know I'll never make a sale once I'm interrupted.'

I think he did the washing for the whole estate that week without a single sale, but it was a delight to see all the curtains and blankets blowing on the washing lines. Housewives are cannier than given credit for!

Family allowance

Every Tuesday we would make our way to the local Post-Office to draw our Family Allowance of eight shillings! (about forty new pence). There was no allowance for the first baby only second and subsequent children. We really looked forward to Tuesday as the money would keep us going until pay-day on Thursday. I think most families had mince-casserole for dinner on Tuesdays, with plenty of vegetables. I shudder to think what rubbish was minced up by the butcher and sold to us so cheaply. My Father-in-law told me I should buy a piece of beef and watch the butcher put it through the mincer as all the left-overs were minced up and sold as 'mince' to make up the profit margins. Another regular outing was to the Church hall on welfare day where we could buy the Government's dried milk and orange juice. The babies would be undressed and weighed and mothers could discuss with the nurse any problems they had regarding baby. When we first moved to Rowner I would take the children to visit my Mother at the week-ends. At first I would catch the bus until the day I had a terrifying experience. I put Sally on the seat just inside the lower deck and returned to the pavement to get the push-chair and Simon … when the bus started to leave the stop! Thankfully one of the passengers realised what was happening and shouted upstairs to the conductor to stop the bus while feverishly ringing the bell. I was very shaken by this and decided from that day on that I would always walk the three miles to visit my Mother. (My hips benefited from the exercise as well.)

Rowner

The housing estate at Rowner was surrounded by countryside, I would push the pram across the golf-course and pick honey-suckle, may-blossom, old man's beard or catkins during our outings, and the children would feed the horses in the field with sugar-lumps or pieces of apple. When Larry had a day off work and the weather was fine, we would pack the bottom of the pram with sandwiches, bottle-feed, rusks, the inevitable supply of nappies and walk three miles through the lanes to the beach at Lee-on-the-Solent. We'd spend the whole day at the seaside, but we had to take turns at swimming in the sea as one of us had to remain with the children on the pebbled beach. Life was very enjoyable.

Interior decoration

The fashion as regards interior decorating makes me cringe when I think about it, the colours in vogue were red, grey and mushroom. We decided to start with painting the dining-room. Neither of us had any previous experience with decorating, and naturally, as any young couple of any generation, we complied with the fashion of the day … grey walls, red painted door surrounds and skirting boards, finished off with mushroom doors. At the time we thought it looked wonderful, toning beautifully with our red formica table and red and black chairs. We decided we were now experienced enough to have a go at hanging wallpaper, my beloved saying he knew the technique of papering a ceiling. We decided we would have the bottom half of the room papered with 'lincrusta' as it would be both serviceable and easy to keep clean. All that would be required was a damp cloth to erase any sticky finger-marks, good thinking with babies in the house. We also thought that when the room needed re-decorating we would only have the top half to re-paper and thereby cut the cost. While Larry was on duty I went to the Crown wallpaper shop in Gosport High Street to buy the paper … big mistake! I didn't ask for it to be trimmed. I didn't know you had to, so while I unrolled each roll of paper Larry carefully trimmed one side and then we repeated the process for the other side, very time consuming. Papering a ceiling for the first time is not a recommended past-time for anyone on a short fuse! I left Larry to do it alone after a couple of lengths of ceiling paper had wrapped themselves around his head, my laughing didn't help … I could see a divorce looming so made a hasty giggling retreat. No sense of humour that one!

My Mother told me she had paid the 'Pearl' insurance company 1d. a week for 21 years in my name and it was now pay-back time … £12! I thought hard about this sudden and unexpected windfall and decided my most pressing need was a vacuum cleaner. Until that moment I had kept the house clean and polished with a broom, mop and dust-pan and brush, a method which re-distributes the dust rather than eliminates it (recycling in today's parlance). New vacuum cleaners were very expensive, so we scanned the 'For Sale' columns of the local paper to find one in our price range. I was a very proud lady as I carried it home for a mile, buoyed along by the fact that house-work would now be a doddle with my magic machine. I think my imagination made it into a miracle appliance but in reality its 'sucking power' was abysmal.

The first Christmas in our new home brought a surprise … a parcel of toys for the children from my Father, it had been re-directed several times, from my Grandmother Silver to my Mother and finally to me. He'd included a letter asking if he could stay for a few days as he would like to keep in contact with me; he'd remarried and lived in Manchester. I asked my Mother what she thought and what I should do. 'Please yourself,' she said, 'It makes no difference to me one way or the other'.

I wrote to thank my Father for the toys and agreed to him coming to stay for a week. My brothers didn't want to meet him but my Mother spent an evening with us and everyone was friendly and relaxed, although not a single word was said about the 1940s. I couldn't find any kind of emotion for this man, he didn't seem like a Father and his new wife, although very friendly, was in fact a total stranger with whom I had absolutely nothing in common. We spent a day

My Father

at Hayling Island but when we looked for somewhere to have lunch it was more difficult than I thought possible. My Father would look into the window of every café and restaurant, shake his head and walk past. 'What's wrong with this one?' I asked as he rejected yet another café. 'I don't go into cafés that have tablecloths' he replied, 'Too posh'.

The children were now getting tetchy, they were hungry and thirsty, their breakfast long forgotten. We finally stumbled upon a place to suit my Father ... a working-mans' café. These were the days before cholesterol became a dangerous thing to have in your blood stream and greasy-spoons were acceptable ... to some! I think at that moment something in my brain told me how great was the gulf between my Mother's and Father's outlooks on life. When the week's holiday came to an end my Father asked if I would keep in touch by post. I said I would. True to his word I received a letter from Manchester. I replied as promised. Then I received a long letter about people I'd never met ... from his wife. I replied to Ada and she wrote back ... I didn't reply. I wrote to Grandmother Silver and explained my disappointment, I had no quarrel with Ada but I thought my Father wanted to make amends for the past. I received a letter from my Father full of apologies and promising to write on a regular basis. I replied ... Ada answered. I didn't write again, neither did he. He died in 1971. My Mother phoned to tell me that she'd heard the news from Grandmother Silver. It meant nothing, to me it was the death of a complete stranger.

Christmas in our own home

Our second Christmas in our own home was better than any I'd previously known, the children were now of an age to appreciate the decorations, tree and presents. We were disturbed all through the night as each child discovered their pillow-case of toys at the end of their respective beds. We decided to change the format next year and leave a stocking on the beds and the rest of the presents downstairs, this way we would at least know who to thank and for what! It was embarrassing to find a pile of screwed up paper and gift-tags strewn all over the bedroom floor and the children happily playing oblivious of the fact that presents given needed a thankyou letter. The two weeks in the run up to Christmas were very exciting. The postman would do a round several times a day delivering his sacks full of cards and in the afternoon a large lorry would deliver the parcels. The post-office was a lucrative time for those who needed extra money for a short period; it recruited an army of casual workers to make sure the mail was delivered on time. Most of the toys on the market were made of plastic. Boys would play with large, brightly coloured cars and lorries for all of five minutes before the wheels fell off. Simon had a 'sit-in' fire engine equipped with ladders and a bell. He played outside on the front path when a group of children surrounded him, I foolishly thought they were admiring his new toy ... I was mistaken. Within a few minutes the fire-engine was totally stripped of every moving part leaving Simon with an ordinary pedal-car. Sally fared better with her dolls and a wooden cot and my Mother had knitted her some doll's clothes, which are much more fiddly to knit than normal size garments.

We made friends with a childless couple. The husband worked with Larry but the wife stayed at home all day, mind you, her hair was always perfect and she told me she had appointments with her hairdresser twice a week … wow! that's what I call luxury! I felt really dull and frumpish. (The hair style now in vogue was a 'bubble-cut', a heaven-sent style for busy mums, the hair would be cut very short and then tightly permed … it was at least two weeks after the perm before the comb could go through it!). Our new friends were fanatical about the game of bridge, so twice a week we had an evening of card playing. To avoid arguments between spouses we exchanged partners. I was relieved as I'd only played Knockout Whist before but at least I knew such terms as trumps, follow suit, renege and the names of the suits. I was more than happy to leave the scoring to the men. These were the days when men liked to show the 'little woman' how superior their intellect was to that of 'wifey', fortunately for them they couldn't read our minds! We would take turns in supplying the food, they always came to our house so that we didn't have the expense of a baby-sitter. The refreshments were simple, crusty bread, salad, raw Spanish onions sliced in vinegar and of course beer to wash it all down. We had some great evenings with this couple which only ended when the husband was drafted abroad.

Friends

In the late 1950s my Mother asked me if I would like to accommodate some friends of hers from Leeds; they wanted a holiday in the Porsmouth area and would I do bed, breakfast and evening meal for them. It sounded easy. Mother had two divan beds that she no longer needed, so if I put the children in our bedroom we could then let them have the other two rooms. They were willing to pay £25 for five people staying two weeks. There was however, one stipulation … we must have a television. Their favourite programme was *Emergency Ward Ten* on ITV and they didn't want to miss any of the episodes while they were on holiday. We didn't own a TV, neither did anyone else that I knew and ITV had only just started to transmit in the Southern Region. We scanned the 'For Sale' columns of the local paper and saw a 12 inch TV for sale at £25. Mother lent us the money which we were to pay back when our visitors had paid for their 'keep'. I'll always remember the first night the TV was installed. Larry was working 'nights', the children were sound asleep and I settled down to watch the late movie, it was called *Lady Hamilton*. Olivier played Nelson, the film was in black and white and continually interrupted by advertisements. The screen was small and the picture quality awful. My eyelids found it increasingly difficult to stay up but although it was past midnight I was determined to watch it through to the bitter end. The next day word had spread around the neighbours that we had a television set and there was a continuous stream of visitors walking in and out of the house … bye bye privacy. No one locked their doors during the day but I was starting to feel that my home was not my own any more.

Bed, breakfast and evening meal

Television

The visitors from Leeds arrived, two ladies, two men and a teenage girl, to start what turned out to be a very, very long fourteen days. Don't misunderstand me, they were lovely people and one of the couples remained friends until they'd both died some 40 years later, but I just hadn't realised the amount of cooking and cleaning involved with so many mouths to feed. I seemed to spend every moment I was not caring for the day-to-day needs of the children at the kitchen sink. I was either preparing meals or washing up and cleaning the house. Larry was understanding enough to live on fried left-overs. I had to make fresh meals for the paying guests but we had no extra money with which to buy the food, it had to be budgeted from the normal week's housekeeping. When the holiday was over and I was paid and profusely thanked for my catering and hospitality, I handed the money over to my Mother for the loan for the TV ... never again!

More furniture

'Divi' time had come round again and we decided to buy a studio-couch, it was a 'must-have' item of furniture ... very in vogue. (We are such slaves to fashion when we're young.) The couches were six feet long, had two large cushions at the back and could be converted into two single beds or one double, most useful. Our living room was slowly beginning to look furnished, we now owned a rug, two armchairs a sideboard and the new couch.

A home perm

One of our neighbours asked if she could 'do' my hair for me. She insisted she was a trained hairdresser before she married, she said she would make me into a blonde and perm my hair all in one go. What a surprise for Larry when he came home from work! Home perms were the latest idea for ladies, they could have their hair curly without the expense of visiting a salon. The hoardings were showing pictures of twin girls with the caption 'Which twin has the Toni? implying that a DIY perm was as good as the real thing. I jumped at the chance of improving my image, who wouldn't? The afternoon was spent bleaching and perming while drinking endless cups of tea and smoking numerous cigarettes. My new friend left me with the curlers in place and wringing wet hair with instructions not to disturb the curlers for at least four hours. The house absolutely reeked of ammonia and just before retiring for the night I decided to unroll the curlers and reveal to Larry the 'new me'. I slowly started to unroll the first curl, but to my dismay and horror when I removed the roller it still had my hair wrapped around it! Then I remembered. A few weeks previous to this I had watched an episode of *I Married Joan* starring Joan Davis on the TV. She had decided to make money by perming hair in the ladies' own homes, but her first attempt left her with the customers hair in the curlers! I thought the programme was hilarious ... in real life it wasn't the slightest bit funny. I lined my hair-covered rollers along the window-sill as I thought of Joan Davis. Funnily enough it turned out to be good for my hair, I had a cap of blond, tight curls covering my head and the ensuing growth was healthier than it had been for years. It was a long, long time before I needed another perm!

I was surrounded by expectant mothers and started to feel broody; logic or common sense did not enter into the equation. Sally was about to start school and a year later Simon would follow. I knew that once the children started school they'd no longer be my babies, it's the first stage of their journey to independence. I would desperately miss the cuddles and unquestioning love that mothers receive from their offspring, but I was facing the cutting of the 'apron-strings', the day they leave the proverbial nest and come under outside influences. Only another woman can understand this feeling of broodiness, when hormones take over every waking thought. There's only one cure for this 'malady' ... get pregnant. Larry didn't understand and suggested we apply to adopt a baby. I said I would like to adopt an eight year old girl as I could empathise with her mental state and feelings at that age. We had an interview and were turned down, which was a bit of a blow to the ego. 'You can only adopt a child who is younger than your own children otherwise it upsets your eldest child.'

I was still broody. Larry finally agreed but only if I could get it all over within the year, he didn't want me to be pregnant from one year into the next. It was November, so I couldn't foresee any problem there. One more condition, a baby or a fur coat for Christmas. This was before Animal Rights made fur coats a taboo item of clothing, a fur coat to a woman was a fashion item to die for (an unfortunate turn of phrase), preferably a mink ... but ladies of my social standing would be happy with a cony fur. I didn't immediately become pregnant, so I thought it would be a good idea to see the doctor, after all it was only four years ago that I couldn't stop being pregnant, so what was the problem? The doctor thought it was funny. I wasn't laughing, but he did think I looked anaemic and took some blood to be tested. I left the surgery none the wiser and with an appointment for the following week when my tests would be back from the lab. I was very anaemic, my blood haemoglobin was so low that I had to start a six-week course of injections straight away.

Broody again

In the winter of 1958 I contracted Asian 'flu, I'd never felt so ill in my life as I did for the next three weeks. My Mother helped with looking after the children but Larry refused to do any household chores on principle. 'If I was meant to do women's work I would have been born wearing an apron!' he told me.

Christmas came and went and we welcomed in the New year. It was now 1959 and I still wasn't pregnant. There was to be a party on New Year's Eve at St. James Hospital in Portsmouth and Larry said we would be going. A new dress was definitely required. I bought a beautiful calf-length dress in sage green taffeta, my hair was now artificially coloured deep auburn (blonde made me look even more anaemic) and the dress complimented my new colouring perfectly. This would be our first social outing since we'd married and I was really looking forward to a night out.

We decided to re-decorate our bedroom for the new year. The process we adopted reminded me of the sitting room at the L's; the walls were emulsioned in pale pink and then a sponge was used to dab a darker shade of pink abstract 'blobs' all over the walls. Perhaps it was looking at the finished article that made me feel ill again.

I went to bed after settling the children for the night, feeling very sorry for myself. The next morning I still felt ill so Larry went to the nearest phone kiosk to ask the doctor if he would call. While I was waiting Larry cooked me some toast and brought it up the stairs. He stood by the side of the bed waving the plate of toast dripping in margarine under my nose. 'If you ate properly you wouldn't keep getting ill. I can't ask for more time off work to look after the children,' he said crossly.

He continued to wave the plate under my nose making me feel so sick that I grabbed a slice of toast and threw it across the room. The doctor walked in just as the butter started to run down the newly painted wall, making a shiny ski run among the pink splotches. He wasn't surprised at my reaction. 'I'm surprised she didn't hit you over the head with the toast,' the Doctor said to Larry. 'Anything greasy will make her sick.' I lived on jelly and porridge oats until the infection had cleared. I'd got a kidney infection.

Larry is promoted

Larry had passed all his exams. and was now an RMN. When he returned to Haslar he was promoted to Petty Officer. To celebrate his new status we were invited to a 'welcome to the mess' social and I really looked forward to dressing up again plus the luxury of a visit to the hairdresser's; any excuse is a good excuse to a woman. At the bottom of Gosport High Street there was a salon in a wooden hut called 'Hills'. The previous establishment had been bombed so this hut was used as a temporary stop-gap. The hairdresser was a young man called John and he was a wizard at seeing which coiffure best suited his female customers, inspecting his client's face from all angles. He decided I would suit a 'Grecian' style, kiss-curls round the face and the hair at the back swept up from the sides to fall in a cascade of curls to the collar ... sounded great. I was telling him how fed up I was with my husband continually talking about a 'pink blonde' who he saw every day on the ferry as he travelled to and from work. 'I will give you pink curls,' he said. 'I'm not sure about that', I said, 'I quite like being auburn.' 'Don't worry,' he replied, 'I'll just spray the ends of each curl with pink, it'll brush out if you don't like it but don't tell your husband that until tomorrow.' Larry was furious with my pink curls ... but he never mentioned the 'blonde' again.

A social outing

The social was both a success and a disaster depending on whose point of view it was. There were loads of silly games with equally silly prizes, but it was during one of the games that I realised how insular I had become since I'd left the Navy. We were playing a game of 'forfeits' and I had to talk for one minute without stopping ... sounds simple enough. I couldn't believe that the most stimulating talk I could produce was to recite nursery rhymes. It was so humiliating! That was the disaster. The success was catching up with all the news and meeting old friends and their wives, I realised how much I missed the fun we used to share. The next day I bought a copy of the *Daily Express*, determined to know exactly what was happening in the world day by day. I also started my love affair with crosswords, a mental life-saver as far as I was concerned. Larry taunted me about everyone I'd spoken to, trying to imply with dark innuendoes that there was more to knowing them than just catching up with old friends. I brushed the 'pink' from my hair and never went to a social function at Haslar again!

April came and I discovered I was pregnant again, yippee! I could always tell if I was pregnant before visiting the doctor because as I'd light my first cigarette of the day it would turn my stomach inside out. It was as simple as that, if I couldn't fancy a ciggy I was pregnant. I told my Mother my good news. 'Oh dear, what a shame, and just as you're getting the children off your hands', she said.

Pregnant again

The staff at the Blake Maternity Home greeted me like an old friend. The only difference I could see was that Matron had retired and Sister was now the Matron. The continuity was very comforting. It was bad news for Larry as the baby would not arrive until January. I was inundated with maternity smocks from my neighbours, they now had their babies and were only too happy to pass the redundant clothes over to me. (You see, we did recycle in the old days, not only dust but clothes as well!)

Sally started school when she was four and a half and Simon was missing her dreadfully, after all she'd always been there. It must have been a similar experience to him as twins being separated. Larry had been drafted on to the *Ark Royal* for a cruise around the Med. and I was secretly enjoying the luxury of pleasing myself about what I could and couldn't do. My neighbours were wonderful and there was always someone to talk to and share a cup of tea. A fourteen-year-old daughter of one of my neighbours would sleep in the house every night just in case the baby decided to arrive early. She would then be on hand to call a taxi for me and arrange for the other two children to go to my Mother's.

During the school's winter term I decided to take Simon to Portsmouth to meet Father Christmas as a special treat. When we finally reached the head of the queue for Santa's Grotto he put up a sign 'Gone to lunch, back at two o'clock'. While I was explaining to Simon that we'd have something to eat and then come back, an elderly gentleman came up to us. 'Why the long face?' he asked Simon. I explained what had happened. 'I'm Santa,' he whispered so that Simon couldn't hear what he was saying. 'Be first in the queue after lunch. I'll write down his name on the palm of my hand and any brothers or sisters he might have.'

Simon meets Father Christmas

I gave him the information and we went to the cafeteria for a sandwich and a milk-shake. An hour later we entered Santa's Grotto. 'Hello Simon, sorry you had to wait,' Santa said, 'I have a special present for you and I also have a gift for you to take home for your sister Sally.' Simon's face was a picture and I knew he would believe in Santa Clause for at least another year.

Simon was due to start school at Easter, exactly a year after Sally, so I had time to spare for the first time in nearly five years. Both the children though had honed in on the fact that Dad was away and Mum was not very agile in her pregnant state. They ganged up on me as only four and five year olds know how. I spotted an ornament in the local hardware shop called a 'fanny-paddle'; it was made of three ply wood, shaped like a cricket bat and only cost 1/6d. I took it home and hung it on a nail on the kitchen wall. There were several ideas written on it, i.e. 'for wives who burn the toast' or 'folks who like to boast' but to me it was a sanity saver. When the children started to 'play-up' I would reach out to take it from the wall and like magic … my little horrors immediately became darling angels. I never actually took it from its nail, it reminded me of Mr Ayres' hamper of canes … a good deterrent. The best 1/6d. I'd ever spent.

Pocket money

I would give the children 2/- each for their weekly pocket money to stop the continuous demands for sweets every time we went into a shop. I would pay for their comics but they had to decide for themselves how they spent their 2/-. Every Thursday I would take the bus to Fareham and Simon would buy a 'Matchbox' car for 1/6d. in Woolworths. The cars were well made and he would play quite happily with his new toy until the following Thursday, when he would buy another. It was years later when I asked him what had happened to all his cars, as in the 1990s 'Matchbox' cars were a desirable collector's item. His reply surprised me. 'Every time I bought a new car I would put the old one in my secret safe,' he said. 'Where was that?' I asked. 'Down the drain outside the house,' he replied, 'It was my secret hiding place.' There's rich pickings in Gosport's sewers!

Blandford

I often took the children to Blandford to visit Aunt May and Uncle Bert. Sometimes for a weekend break or, during school holidays we'd stay for two weeks. We were all thoroughly spoilt. Both my Aunt and Uncle were Godparents to Simon and they doted on both children. I had a Pembrokeshire Corgi, which Larry bought me before he went away, two children to look after and a new baby on the way. I was happier than I had ever been before in my life. I could practise my cake baking and jam making without fear of criticism.

Larry said he wanted another daughter and we'd call her Kate. I had a son in January and called him Martin (Warlike) John (Jehovah is Gracious). The birth was not straight forward.

'Don't push, don't push', the nurses kept shouting at me.

I'd been here twice before and I knew that the harder you pushed the quicker it was over, although there did seem to be more staff in the labour ward than I remembered having before. I must have dozed off after all my exertions as the next thing I remembered was the Doctor standing in the delivery room and a strange snuffling sound coming from the corner. 'Where's my baby?' I snapped. I admit I was feeling a trifle ratty and any thoughts of politeness had flown out of the window. 'He's asleep in the cradle', the doctor replied. 'There's something wrong' I grumbled. 'I haven't seen him or held him yet and I haven't even had a cup of tea'.

I knew the routine, have baby, cuddle baby, have a cup of tea and a biscuit

… then sleep. I was doing everything in reverse and was scared the baby was damaged. The Doctor and Matron exchanged glances and the Doctor nodded. Matron went to the corner of the room and held up a purple bundle and just as quickly put it back.

'He's black,' I sobbed, not at all reassured by the glimpse I'd had of my newborn, he was a dark blob swathed in white. 'He's just a little short of oxygen that's all,' the Doctor assured me.

A few days after Martin was born a large bouquet of flowers arrived and everyone assumed they were from my husband … they were from Aunt May, but I didn't tell anyone. I had a friend, Ida, who would visit me every evening regardless of the cold and rain. She appeared each night without fail even though she had four children of her own to look after. In 1960 the stay in the nursing home was ten days not fourteen days as before.

When I returned home Ida had lit the boiler to warm the kitchen, lit the paraffin heater in the living-room and laid out nappies and baby clothes to welcome my new arrival; she was a true friend. Again I realised how lucky I was to have such kind neighbours and two incidents stay in my mind. The first incident was when it had snowed heavily overnight and the man next door had swept my path before I'd even started my day; the second incident saved my sanity. It had been raining for almost five days non-stop and the wet washing was piling up, when suddenly the moon came out and a strong wind blew the rain clouds away. I stood in the dark garden pegging out a long line of washing, but as I returned to the kitchen I heard a loud cracking sound … my line had broken and my clean washing was lying in the mud. I wanted to sit down and howl, more with frustration than anger, but instead I walked to a neighbour's kitchen where I knew there was always a welcome cup of tea.

'What's up?', she asked, as she sent her daughter to my house to sit with the children until I returned. 'I put the washing out and the line snapped,' I wailed. 'I can't face it at the moment. I'll have a cup of tea and a cigarette before I start washing it all again.' 'Sit yourself down and don't worry,' she said.

When I returned home half an hour later the dirty washing was in the kitchen and my line had been repaired by her husband. Priceless neighbours. The young teenager would visit each evening and we would laugh at the new Antony Newley series on TV called *Guerney Slade*. The plot was inside a human brain and all the messages sent by the body to the brain, it was inventive and hilarious.

I enjoyed having the children to myself and I worked out a routine for each child

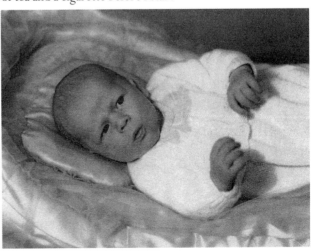

to have a fair share of Mum's attention. While Sally was at school, Simon had my undivided attention once Martin had been bathed and fed in the mornings and I always made sure that I sat with Simon on the studio couch while Martin had his lunch-time bottle. We'd watch *Bill and Ben*, *Tales of the River Bank* and *Picture Book*. One lunch-time, just before it was time for *Watch with Mother* I noticed Simon staring intently at a cow giving birth on the TV. My initial reaction was to turn the set off, but I'm very glad I hesitated. 'Is that how Martin was born?' he asked. Exactly like that,' I said.

There was no further comment, he'd accepted what he'd seen as a natural occurrence. When Sally came home from school I would give her as much time as she needed and after she and Simon were tucked up for the night it was Martin's time. I think I was lucky as Martin slept most of the day but was fully awake during the evenings. It suited the family routine beautifully. I'd started to make cakes and laughed at my first batch of charcoal edged chocolate cakes, which reminded me of my Mother's cakes at Brockhurst. We walked down the lanes and harvested the wild blackberries to make apple and blackberry jam. I can almost taste it now, Hovis bread and butter covered in home-made apple and blackberry jam ... delicious. I was slowly gaining confidence with my culinary skills and looking forward to surprising Larry with my new-found talents when he came home from his travels.

Writing to Larry

I think I had more conversations with Larry while he was away from home than when we were together. We would write letters by return of post; we'd agreed before he sailed not to write everyday as it causes one to worry if a letter doesn't arrive when expected. He would tell me about the parties in the Wrens' messes which the 'ship's company' was invited to when they were in harbour; places he'd seen, ports his ship visited and people he'd met during his trips ashore. Added to this he was enjoying a cruise round the Mediterranean. He visited Italy, Malta, Gibraltar and Greece, but I could only write about the mundane happenings at home. I'd try to make each small incident more interesting than it actually was in an effort to fill the pages and give him something to read. One example of this was 'The Mouse'. I was watching TV one evening after the children were all safely tucked up in bed, when I heard scratching noises coming from the ceiling. At first I thought it was a bird on the roof, but soon realised this wasn't possible as there was another room between the ceiling and the tiles. I mentioned it to my friend and she said it was possibly mice between the floorboards and she'd ask her husband to have a look when he came home at the weekend. It appeared that the mice had somehow nested between the floorboards, so a trap was set on Friday night and a dead mouse taken out Saturday morning. This was repeated every weekend for several weeks until the trap ceased to provide any corpses. I thought that if I embroidered the incident it would make for more interesting reading than 'the kids have measles or Martin's latest weight gain when I took him to see the Welfare nurse'

My brother David, his wife Marion plus their two children travelled from Boscombe Down to spend Easter with us. We'd planned to visit HMS *Victory* during Navy days. Visits to the dockyard and *Victory* were free in those days and made an interesting and informative outing for the children. We decided to go on Bank Holiday Monday, but as I was dressing Sally I noticed some blisters on her neck … she had chickenpox. David and Marion took Simon with their two children while Sally, Martin and I stayed at home. Sally had to stay away from other children for three weeks, which meant missing the first week of the new term at school. Simon however, started his first day in the Infants' and walked by the side of the pram quite looking forward to his first day at school. That evening, while I was washing him I noticed a blister on his neck … he had chickenpox. I was slightly concerned for Martin as he was only four months old, but the Doctor assured me he would be safe at his age. I'd kept the other two children away from him while they were infectious so he should be okay. Exactly six weeks after first sighting Sally's blister, Martin was covered in spots! The Doctor said he wasn't surprised as it had been a particularly vicious out-break that year. I felt as if I'd been quarantined myself for six weeks, all my friends had children of their own which meant our family was a 'no-go' area.

Larry abroad

When I read about the places Larry was visiting I started to get itchy-feet and wishing we could get an accompanied draft and travel together. I saw an advertisement for a two- week cruise round the Mediterranean for £12. I thought I could save for that and Larry could look after the children while I went away for a much needed rest. I cut the advert from the paper and put it away in a drawer with my savings until my beloved came home. I had mixed emotions about Larry's return home, he had expressed emotions and feelings in his letters that he'd never shown in the seven years we'd been married – they were the kind of letters written by courting couples. I wasn't sure which direction our relationship would take as the writer of the letters seemed a totally different person to the man I'd lived with before his trip abroad. I was determined though to look my best when we met again and took a great deal of trouble and care buying a new outfit and treating myself to a new hair-do. I arranged for us to go out with our neighbours for the second evening he was home as I thought it would be an opportunity for him to meet the 'mouse-catcher'. I was not prepared for his comments when I told him who we were going out with. He accused me of having an affair! I couldn't believe that he could even think such a thing. It ruined a good friendship as I was afraid to look or speak to my friends in case Larry read something into an innocent look or word that was only a figment of his imagination. The 'new-man' who wrote to me was now the 'old-man' back from his travels … nothing had changed for the better. It could have been funny if it hadn't been so sad. The opportunities to have affairs when a husband was at sea were numerous, it seemed to me that every male tradesman who called at the door propositioned me, only to be firmly knocked back. I told Larry about the money I'd saved and showed him the advert, 'Over my dead body,' he said. I bought new china, sent out invitations to everyone I could think of and Martin had the best Christening party ever! Larry also thought *Guerney Slade* was a load of rubbish.

Max, the corgi

I had an unexpected problem with Max, the corgi dog. He was a proper lap dog and during my pregnancy would spend each evening curled up on my lap like a baby. After the arrival of Martin, Max's whole attitude changed. When I picked the baby out of his pram Max would stand in a pose similar to that of a pointer and growl his disapproval. This was worrying, it meant I couldn't leave Martin unattended when I left the room in case Max bit him. When Aunt May and Uncle Bert came for Martin's Christening I told them of my fears and Uncle Bert said he would love to have Max, so Max went to Blandford. I'll do a quick jump ahead five years while I'm mentioning Max. (It's not really a tangent … honest!). Aunt May and Uncle Bert came to stay in 1965 and bought Max with them. He jumped all over me, Sally and Simon, his little stump of a tail wagging so fast it looked as if it would fall off. He bit Martin! Dogs must have similar memory banks to elephants!

We'd decided the time had come to buy our own home, the way council rents went up with every pay rise meant we'd be better off financially with a mortgage. Our credit limit would be £2,000, as £200 was the maximum we could scrape together for the deposit. After searching in both Fareham and Gosport we found a house to suit, but it was £200 more than we could afford. We made an appointment to see the bank-manager with a long list of items we thought essential, hoping for a loan. The list contained items such as beds, tables, carpets and a washing machine until we finally made the total add up to the £200 shortfall. We reasoned that the bank-manager wasn't to know we already owned most of the furniture on the list. I'd managed without a washing machine up to now and Martin had finished with nappies so it wasn't really that essential. We nervously sat in the Manager's office while he silently scrutinised our requirements.

No washing machine

'You don't need a washing machine,' he said, briefly looking up from the list in his hand, 'My wife's had seven children and manages perfectly well with a boiler and a wringer.' He must have thought he read the disappointment on our faces. Actually we were thinking what a mean husband he must be and felt sorry for this poor lady at home, with her seven children to care for and no modern appliances to make her life easier.

'There's only one way to stay out of debt,' he told us. 'You can only pay out each month on a mortgage what you earn in one week.' He agreed to loan us half of what we'd asked, but in retrospect we were grateful – a larger loan would have stretched us beyond our means.

Our own home

I think the decision to buy the house we eventually decided on was entirely due to the fact that it had a refrigerator in the kitchen … what luxury! The new house didn't have an airing-cupboard though, so we bought a 'Flatly Drier' to air the piles of ironed clothes. An added bonus was the fact that it warmed the kitchen at the same time, making it very cosy. It was a very short-lived house-hold appliance. Larry received a payment of £25 for signing on after he had completed twelve years' service, the electric bill arrived the same day ... it was £25! The Flatly left home *tout de suite*.

We'd only been in our new home a couple of months when David and Marion invited us to stay with them for two weeks on the Isle of Wight. David was in the RAF and they were lucky enough to have a married quarter at Ventnor. They had two children and expecting their third child that winter. It was a beautiful place to stay, right on the top of the Downs and I soon realised how unfit I had become. After a couple of days walking down to the beach my calves were so painful I didn't know what to do with them ... at the end of the holiday I was walking up and down the hills like a native. The cliff path was so steep that we put the brake on Martin's pushchair and pulled it behind us, but the weather was kind and we returned home much fitter than when we'd left 14 days previously.

The Isle of Wight

The first morning after our holiday, Simon appeared at breakfast covered in strange spots but he showed no signs of being unwell. Larry looked concerned. 'We need to examine his bed, come upstairs quickly,' he said. I didn't understand but followed him to the boy's bedroom. The wall and bed were a mass of strange insects. 'What on earth are they?' I asked. 'Bed-bugs', said Larry. ' How did they get here?' I asked, 'Do I have to phone the council to have the rooms fumigated?' 'I'm not having the neighbours know we have them,' Larry replied, 'I'll get some powder from the Hospital to put under all the floor-boards. The bed will have to be burnt, we'll have a bonfire tonight when I come home from work'.

True to his word Larry came home with the powder and we burnt the beds in the garden. We tore up all the lino from the floor and burnt that as well. Larry took up the floorboards and lavishly sprinkled the tins of powder in every gap and crevice. I had never heard of bed-bugs in my life and it came as quite a shock. Even to this day, nearly 50 years later, I still check for bugs when I make the beds, it's as natural to me as breathing. Not an experience I would like repeated.

Another thing that I found quite disturbing was the number of flies that would appear each evening on the kitchen ceiling. I didn't think it was possible that they just happened to like our kitchen at night, but the ceiling was black with a heaving mass of them every night without fail. I scrubbed, I cleaned, still they were there every night. One wall was covered in an attractive red pin-board and as a last resort to solve the mystery I asked Larry if we should remove it. We did remove it. The wall underneath it was thick with grease. I tried to penetrate it with some hot water and 'Flash' but it wouldn't budge. I then applied neat 'Flash' on a cloth and finally managed to clean the wall. The flies disappeared overnight. Do others understand when I ask the question ... 'Why do I always have the previous occupier's mess to clear up, when I always leave my house so clean for its new owner?'

The kitchen must now be redecorated. We chose a blue and white 'willow-patterned' wallpaper for the walls and tiled the floor in a dark and light blue diamond pattern. We were well pleased with the result. Larry also decided to completely refurbish the kitchen. He asked me to stand against the wall so that he could build all the surfaces to suit my height. I had a made-to-measure kitchen with plenty of cupboard space … it was very, very good The icing on the top of the cake … Larry bought me a Rolls twin-tub washing machine for my birthday.

The first man in space

We lived through two earth-shattering events during the 1960s so I thought I would record the feelings of ordinary folk on these occasions. The first was a huge leap in science. Yuri Gagarin made the first manned flight in space on the 12 April 1961. 'Oh my God' was my reaction. I found it very scary and thought it was the first step towards Armageddon. If the scientists started mucking about with our solar system we were surely heading for destruction.

The second event was the assassination of John F. Kennedy. It's said that everyone remembers where they were when the news broke. We were nowhere in particular, just at home and settling down for an evening's TV viewing. Our reaction, ' Oh my God, we're about to witness the start of World War III'. It was a frightening prospect, but we really believed that Kennedy was the man to stand up to any threats from Russia … what now we wondered?

'Pop' music

I know there were other events in the 1960s. The ' pop' music was vibrant, Beatles music was being played on every Radio Station and contrasting with the heavier sounds of the Rolling Stones. Pop Festivals were 'must go there' venues for the youngsters. There was ' Flower Power' and Hippies. We saw the beginning of the Mods and Rockers, spoiling family excursions to the beach on Bank Holidays. Mary Quant lifted our hemlines above the decency level and

tights replaced stockings at the same time as males thought the ladies were sexually liberated … the tights shut the door! But I was an old married lady in her thirties and not really a part of all the new crazes. My mother had re-married and was living happily in New Zealand near Gerald and Joy was in Norway, so once again the family was scattered all over the place.

We had another son, Matthew (Gift of God) Charles (Manly) Edward (Happy Guardian) in 1969 making our family complete. I now felt totally secure, our own home, no wars, no rationing and enough money coming in each week for us not to worry.

After 17 years of marriage Larry left home and we subsequently divorced. There's not a lot of interest in the years that followed as it's so commonplace nowadays to be left as a single mother and cope the best you know how, although I do regret that my children didn't have better parents. I re-married and divorced, then re-married. When I have to put my signature to a document or cheque I sometimes have to hesitate to think of my current name. I think men have an advantage there as they keep one name regardless of the number of times they change partners. Me? ... I'm just mixed up!

I still believe that the most important thing a parent can give a child is a 'childhood'. Once that has been damaged the result is a damaged adult. I'm not vain enough to say that I gave my children a perfect upbringing ... but I did my best.

THE END

POSTSCRIPT

I've recently applied for my first passport at the ripe old age of sixty-six. After sending for a birth certificate and receiving an adoption certificate, I realise that I didn't exist between 1933 and 1941. My life started on that traumatic day in Salisbury. Old as I am, I still find it very painful to accept that I was born at the age of eight-and-three-quarters.

Joan Hide